Faithful Education

Faithful Education

Themes and Values for Teaching, Learning, and Leading

edited by
AMY LYNN DEE AND GARY TIFFIN

☙PICKWICK *Publications* · Eugene, Oregon

FAITHFUL EDUCATION
Themes and Values for Teaching, Learning, and Leading

Pickwick Publications
An Imprint of Wipf and Stock Publishers
199 W. 8th Ave., Suite 3
Eugene, OR 97401

www.wipfandstock.com

ISBN 13: 978-1-62032-249-9

Cataloguing-in-Publication data:

Faithful education : themes and values for teaching, learning, and leading / edited by Amy Lynn Dee and Gary Tiffin ; foreword by Patrick Allen.

xviii + 158 pp. ; 23 cm. Includes bibliographical references.

ISBN 13: 978-1-62032-249-9

1. Education. 2. Effective Teaching. 3. Educational leadership. I. Dee, Amy Lynn. II. Tiffin, Gary (Gerald C.). III. Allen, Patrick. IV. Title.

LB1072 F22 2012

Manufactured in the U.S.A.

*The editors and contributors dedicate this book
to all of our students who enrich our lives and practice,
and to the Dean of the George Fox University School of Education,
Linda Samek, who inspires, supports, and believes.*

Faith is to believe what we do not see;
and the reward of this faith is to see what we believe.

—Saint Augustine

Contents

Contributors

Rebecca A. Addleman is Associate Professor of Education, George Fox University, Portland Center, Oregon. Her seventeen-year career in education includes experience teaching at every level. Her recent publications include: "Transformative Learning Through Cultural Immersion"; and (with C. Brazo and T. Cevallos) "Developing Pre-service Teachers' Attitudes Toward Diversity: Narratives of MAT Students Abroad."

Ken Badley is Professor of Education, George Fox University, Newberg, Oregon. He has taught at the secondary, undergraduate, and graduate levels in public and private settings in Canada and the United States. He serves as book review editor for the *Journal of Education and Christian Belief*. Recent publications include: *The Metaphors We Teach By*, edited with Harro van Brummelen; and "Where does Faith-Learning Integration Happen?," in *Faith Integration for Schools of Education*, edited by Maria Pacino and Marsha Fowler.

Ginny D. Birky is Professor of Education, George Fox University, Newberg, Oregon. She taught for eighteen years at the secondary level. Her publications include "Revisiting Teacher Leadership: Perceptions of Teachers and Principals" and "Spotlight on Success: What's Working in Oregon High Schools?"—a series of ten documents available on Oregon's Department of Education website.

Amy Lynn Dee is NCATE Coordinator and Assistant Professor of Education at George Fox University, Newberg, Oregon. She has worked in public education as a teacher and administrator. Her recent publications include "Evidence of Cultural Competence within Teacher Performance Assessment"; "Preservice Teacher Application of Differentiated Instruction"; and "Creating an Educational Ethos where Innovation and Accountability

Flourish: A New Model for Transparency in Educational Organizations" with Ken Badley.

Gary M. Kilburg is Director of the Mentoring Institute and Professor of Education, George Fox University, Newberg, Oregon. He has been an educator for over forty-three years and has served as a board member for the International Mentoring Association. He has published in *Mentoring and Tutoring Journal, Teachers College Record*, and *ICCTE Journal*.

Terah R. Moore is Assistant Professor of Education, George Fox University, Boise Center, Idaho. She taught as a bilingual classroom teacher at the elementary level. Her recent dissertation is "A Governance Examination of Idaho's Technological Literacy Policy and Standards for Teachers: Past, Present, and Future."

Marc Shelton is Professor of Education, George Fox University, Newberg, Oregon. His career began in public school system where he worked for seventeen years prior to higher education. He serves on the executive board of NCPEA. Recent publications include "Improving Schools: Studies in Leadership and Culture"; "The Evolution of ORPEA: Collaborating to Prepare High Quality Leaders"; and "An Administrator's Challenge: Encouraging Teachers to Be Leaders."

Gary Tiffin is Associate Professor of Education and Director of the doctoral program in education, George Fox University, Newberg, Oregon. His forty-three year career in Christian higher education has included teaching history and social science courses and serving as Chief Academic Officer of two universities. His publications include: "Why We Will Not Lose Our Light: How Can Our Colleges Flourish in a Changing World"; "Disciples Higher Education: 19th Century roots and 21st Century Concerns"; and "Women and the Problem of Credulity," in *Women and Earliest Christianity* edited by Carroll Osborne.

Shary Wortman is Assistant Professor of Education, George Fox University, Redmond Center, Oregon. She has served as a teacher, counselor, and administrator in a public school system and has taught numerous courses at the university level.

Foreword

WHEN I THINK OF faithful teachers, I think of Mrs. Regan. Mrs. Regan was my fourth-grade teacher, and for some reason we didn't hit it off very well. I don't remember much of what happened in class that year, but I do remember that as I was leaving class on the last day of school, I turned to her as she was standing in the doorway and said, "Mrs. Regan, I didn't like this class and I don't like you!" I didn't think much about that mean-spirited comment until I found out that Mrs. Regan had been moved to the fifth grade. Yikes! When I came to class on the first day, Mrs. Regan asked me if I remembered saying anything to her as I left her fourth-grade classroom last spring. I said, "no," mainly because I didn't know what else to say. She smiled at me and said, "I don't remember either." What a gift of grace she gave to me that day.

She told my mother years later that she was determined to make a connection with me so she asked me if I would be her "Science Assistant," an assignment consisting of helping to set up and tear down science experiments and clean the blackboards after school. We talked about how much fun science was, and as I look back, it was at that time that learning became fun for me. Every time I teach research methods to graduate students I think of Mrs. Regan. And every time I remain gracious in the midst of meanness and ingratitude, I thank Mrs. Regan.

I think of Mrs. Matson, my high school literature teacher. She was a wonderful teacher—so full of passion for literature, for her students, and for life. She invited three of us, all athletes, to go sailing with her one Saturday, and we jumped at the chance. While sailing on Lake Michigan, she looked me square in the eye and told me that she thought I was smarter than I let on, and it wasn't a bad thing to like school as well as sports. In fact, she admired folk who were passionate about all aspects of their lives. "It could be," she said, "that you are just as gifted as a thinker as you are an athlete. Why hide your gifts? You try to be your best you can be on the basketball court; why not be your best in my classroom, too?" It was a watershed moment for me. She let me know that it was cool to be good in school. She gave me courage to step beyond the social constraints and peer pressures to do my best in every class, to enjoy learning, and to show it. She didn't want me to let the opinions of my peers define my beliefs and behaviors. Every time I speak to athletes on campus, guess what I tell them.

I think of Dr. Bell, my college psychology professor. When I think of his classes, all I remember is love. He loved to teach, he loved psychology, he loved his wife, he loved his family, he loved the university, he loved having us over to his house, he loved to meet with us in his office, he loved it when we did well on our quizzes, and he loved us—even when we didn't do so well. And we loved him! I majored in psychology because of Dr. Bell. That kind of passion, authenticity, and acceptance are contagious. He taught his students much more than just psychology—how to be a good marriage partner, how to love your family, how to love learning, how to express your feelings, how to pray and how to love your neighbor. He modeled for me what it meant to be a Christian, and to this day, he remains a mentor—even though I haven't talked to him in more than thirty years.

And I think of Dr. Sharp, my favorite teacher and doctoral advisor. He was extremely demanding, and about half way through my first semester of doctoral work, he asked me to stop by his office for a chat. He was holding one of my papers, and he asked me if that paper represented my best work. Well, I told him, it was probably not my absolute best work, but it was pretty good—especially considering that I was working full time while going to school, I wasn't getting a lot of sleep, I was traveling quite a bit, and I was teaching a large young adult Sunday School class at my church. He looked at me, smiled, and said, "I don't want you to submit anything to me but your very best work—ever. You show respect to me when you do that and you show respect for yourself, too. One of the highest acts of worship is to make your desk an altar—and that requires intellectual excellence. You are not called to be a mediocre thinker or writer." Wow! From that day on, he received nothing but my best work, and the same was true for all my professors. Now as a university provost, I often have the privilege to speak to honor society inductees and scholarship recipients. I always tell them about Dr. Sharp, and the call to honor God with your mind.

From my teachers, I certainly learned the lessons of the day, but I learned so much more. I learned about grace, humility, honestly, hospitality, the call to excellence, and love. Beyond the lessons of the day, these were life lessons—matters of spirit and faith. In *Faithful Education*, you will read about matters of spirit and faith, how teachers build bridges that students walk across. Two important tasks for students are to bridge culture and faith and to bridge faith and knowledge. Students need to think carefully about how they are shaped by their culture and how they practice their faith, and exactly what their faith has to say to the prevailing culture. If students are to understand how to live as a faithful presence in their culture, they will need role models and mentors. You will find good examples in this book.

And students need guidance and support if they are to think carefully about their faith and learning, and how to learn faithfully. Deep Christian faith and a rigorous pursuit of knowledge are not only compatible; they are inseparable. Students need teachers who will help them see and understand that Christian faith and knowledge are never at odds. Rather, like two sides of the same coin, they are supportive and complementary. They are equally necessary. Faith without knowledge is full of passion, but lacks substance and depth—difficult to sustain for a lifetime. Knowledge without faith is ultimately dangerous—lacking a reliable guidance system for the intellectual journey. I trust that the chapters of this book will provide readers with guidance and encouragement for the great task of teaching, shaping, and sending.

Patrick Allen, PhD
Provost, George Fox University

Acknowledgments

THE EDITORS WISH TO thank all contributing authors for their energetic participation and collegiality. It has been a joy to work with all of them in this endeavor. We also extend our gratitude to the George Fox University Faculty Development Committee for the support received. Last, we thank our spouses, Andrew Dee and Pat Tiffin for their unending love, encouragement, and patience.

Preface

AMY LYNN DEE *and* GARY TIFFIN

THIS COMPENDIUM OF ESSAYS is presented by nine faculty members of the School of Education at George Fox University in Newberg, Oregon. The authors represent a cross-section of the fifty faculty who serve some 700 current and future teachers, principals, superintendents, and other administrators. They teach in MAT, MEd., EdD, Administrative Licensure, and undergraduate teacher preparation programs. The following essays evidence experience and insight arising from both teaching and administration, as well as experience in K–12 and higher education settings. We encouraged each author to address themes presented through their own voice and out of their own experience. Hence, the essays presented are diverse in style, metaphor, and perspective, even as each purposes to connect biblical faith and practice to significant values, ideals, and practices associated with education.

The title "Faithful Education" connotes education as a foundation of Christian faith, as well as intentional passion for effective teaching, learning and leading. The two sides of this title can be understood even more specifically.

- Faithful as rooted in Christian belief, worldview, and frame of reference.
- Faithful as reliably committed to the ideals; shared purposes; and canons of effective teaching, learning and leading.
- Faithful as committed to student growth, success, and integrity as true measures of effective practice.

- Faithful as referring to the profession of education, even to the point of claiming a sense of "calling" as a fundamental foundation of that faithfulness.

- Faithful as understanding that careers in education must include continuing growth, a sense of process as content, and a dynamic that promotes innovation and creativity.

- Faithful as embracing assessment, evaluation, and continuing improvement as a necessary ingredient for effective education.

We recognize that educators who do not share our Christian faith usually share many if not all of the "faithful factors" identified above. Most educators likely embrace the themes and values addressed in the chapters ahead. We believe that each is rooted and grounded in biblical truth, example, and frame of reference. It is our expectation then that this volume can serve many sectors of the education profession within the Christian community and beyond. It is our hope that anyone in the field of education will find challenge, provocation, and refreshment in these essays, in the continuing effort to improve the practice of teaching and leading in our time.

1

Grace

Amy Lynn Dee

THERE WAS A LARGE coatroom in the back of the class, perfect for storing the boots and coats required in the winter days of my third year in school. It also served as a great place to hide if math was not of particular interest. Mrs. Callahan, realizing she was missing a difficult and resistant math student, kept teaching as she made her way to the door of the coatroom to take the hideaway, Arthur, by surprise. She pushed the door open, and as she entered to sweep aside the hanging coats in order to reveal the missing student, Arthur, who had tricked her, came out from his hiding place behind the door and swiftly closed it, locking a startled Mrs. Callahan on the other side. Craning our necks toward the back of the room, all 29 of us watched in stunned silence as our imprisoned red-faced teacher demanded, through the window of the coatroom door, that Arthur let her out. Frozen by the fear of what he had just done, Arthur stood rooted to the gray linoleum and began to wail at the top of his lungs. At just the right time, the custodian came by with his ring of keys and unlocked the door freeing Mrs. Callahan. What happened next reflected nothing other than pure grace. Mrs. Callahan scooped up the sobbing Arthur and held him close until he stopped crying, and we all listened as she told this very challenging child that she loved him still. No yelling, no threats, no sitting in a chair facing the corner. A prolonged silence followed this simple gift of grace that remains, to this day, one of my strongest memories of God's unmistakable presence and influence in a public elementary classroom.

Miraculous accounts of deaths rescinded, magnificent stories of truths revealed, and memorable narratives of leaders and followers bind us to an ancient era and captivate both those who study Scripture in a faithful and scholarly manner, as well as those who peruse verses on occasion; but regardless of the purpose for reading Scripture, the concept of grace alone serves to confound those of us who lay no claim to exegetical expertise and perhaps even to those who study the earliest Aramaic manuscripts. Years ago, on the way to see the Grand Canyon, I read a guidebook that said no words existed in the English language to describe the size of this fracture in the earth. Upon looking into the canyon for the first time, I thought of the guidebook and knew that the absence of words to describe this wonder made it incomprehensible even though it was right in front of my eyes. To wrestle with the notion that God loved his creation with an entirely incomprehensible fullness and offered Jesus as an acquittal so that all who believe in Him have a promise of everlasting life regardless of righteousness, brings us face to face with an plan so enormous in its grace that we can not help but wonder if it is real. We do not have to prove our worthiness; we only have to believe. Even when we stand frozen in fear at the realization of our unworthiness, grace alone ties us to the heart of God and allows us an intimate experience with the mystery and wonder of the greatest gift ever given. How do we respond to this gift of grace as educators and scholars? Can we attach words to this gift in order that it become comprehensible so that we might explain it and embody it in ways that honor God and encourage colleagues and students?

Paul tells us in Romans 3:24 that we are "justified freely by God's grace through the redemption that came by Christ Jesus." Our early Sunday School lessons taught us that the crucifixion of Jesus atones for the sins of all women and men, and our faith in Jesus as our Savior allows for eternal heavenly life. We do not have to sit in a corner in shame because Jesus hung on a cross in pain. While it sounds simple: we all sin and we are all forgiven, God's gift of grace through Jesus, while not demanding good works for the entrance into God's presence, does imply organically that we respond to the gift with gratitude demonstrated through our living as Christians. Redemption comes through Jesus as an act of grace, but we accept that Grand Canyon sized grace as a people following the moral imperatives embedded in hearts that recognize Christ as God, teacher, role model and redeemer.

The biblical definition of grace remains one that provides Christians with great hope, yet some scholars argue that the concept of grace allows some to discard God as the ultimate heavenly judge. William Muehl in *The Living Pulpit* (January–March 1995) asserts that the concept of grace is grossly misused among Christians who lead decadent permissive lifestyles in reliance upon God's forgiveness. Muehl denounces those who use grace as an excuse to forego the commandments given in Scripture, and reminds us that the concept of grace must remain within the larger story of God and creation (see Romans 6:1–11). While Muehl manages to remove the wonder and joy from the gift of grace, he does elevate the gift with the statement, "Grace neither precedes nor follows from good works. It permeates the whole spectrum of divine action in history, giving what might be called texture to each human experience" (p. 17). While not incumbent upon good work, grace does indeed require a type of good work not addressed by Martin Luther that appears in action and gratitude.

Of course, the Arthur of my childhood knew he had done wrong. The realization that he had locked his teacher in a coatroom without seeing a way to redemption prompted a meltdown that Mrs. Callahan immediately saw as a cry of fear, humility, and complete surrender to the hands and heart of one more powerful. Our submission to God coupled with our acceptance of grace implies a tacit agreement to act as agents of grace, ourselves. Grace is not a stand-alone as a biblical concept, but ties to humility, acceptance, responsibility, forgiveness, joy, and gratitude; all themes addressed in other chapters within this book. Christians who recognize and acknowledge the magnitude of the gift of grace have little choice but to live as Christ desires of us and to reflect his work in ours. How can we not respond to the gift of grace as humble servants ready to reciprocate through sincere action as the hands and feet of Christ?

Grace, as commonly defined, denotes a fluidity and elegance in movement, a state of goodwill, and a well-mannered disposition, all of which suit educators very well. One might define physical grace as the Russian ballerina, Anna Pavlova's performance in Giselle, or even wide receiver Jerry Rice speeding toward the end zone, but almost no one considers as grace the deftness by which a teacher moves in between subjects, standards, objectives, and a multitude of questions while navigating over spilled backpacks and through chair legs and extension cords. A Mother Teresa or Ghandi-like desire for goodwill brings world-wide recognition for a few, but not for those who work to help the underprivileged on a daily basis in the country's most difficult classrooms, and do so with a sincere desire to make a difference. Finally, a pleasant and charming temperament, perceived by both students and their parents, can make or break the success of a teacher in most communities. Given the complexity of education today, a teacher without the attributes of the common definition of grace will not fare well in the field at all. One with the common attributes of grace might very well find success, but one with both the common attributes of grace and who also embodies the biblical concept of grace in attitude and action will most certainly find success as measured by professional standards, and by lives forever transformed by an educator who brought the presence of God into a classroom.

Even though God's grace comes with no strings attached, teachers who not only discern the Christ that dwells within students, but who also appreciate the human frailty and vulnerability of those same students, may more aptly accept and respond to all students, including the Arthurs of our day, with more grace than those teachers who are blinded by a mindset that students will get only what they deserve within a classroom or institution without bearing any responsibility for their growth as a scholar and human being. We have been blessed by a grace far greater than we deserve, and if we are willing to accept that grace, we must in turn, take these definitions and reflect grace within our practice. The remainder of the chapter focuses upon the manifestation of grace in our classrooms and institutions.

GRACE IN PEDAGOGY

Outside forces and inside realities converge to create the working climate and school culture in which teachers enact the call to teach. The work can feel overwhelming. Grace in practice, or specifically grace in pedagogy, unites the professional requirements and expectations of teachers with the academic targets and required behavior of students resulting in praxis that exemplifies championship teaching. Legislation, changing standards, accreditation organizations, grassroots community groups, policy makers, teacher licensing agencies, parent groups, and students themselves all apply an oft undue measure of pressure to a job that already demands that each teacher hold an arsenal of strategies and methods to teach the gifted along side those who struggle with learning, a relational disposition in order to work with all children and their parents or guardians, a collaborative nature so that professional interactions lead to student achievement and breadth of knowledge in the content areas. The heroic among educators handle these demands and expectations with finesse and acceptance. The graceful teachers handle such demands with finesse and acceptance, and they also keep the bureaucracy and the stress of the current culture toward education out of the learning environment. These teachers teach as if the only thing that mattered was student achievement and they work outside the tangle of politics to ensure that all students learn.

Student learning, the ultimate goal in any educational system, remains the imperative of all schools, but fulfilling the mandate has become more challenging for even the most gifted teachers. Our classrooms, no longer marked by industrial age homogeneity, contain the richness and blessing of diversity along with the monumental challenge to reach all learners. Differentiation, a practice introduced by Tomlinson (1999) asks teachers to vary methods, student products, and assessments based on student need. Instead of a "one size fits all" lesson plan, teachers plan for each student in the classroom. Honoring the individual learning style of each student through careful planning, and some individualized instruction paired with allowing students different methods by which they demonstrate knowledge, illustrates grace in action. The flexibility that encourages and assists each student in meeting curricular objectives respects the uniqueness of the individual. When faced with a student who challenges a teacher's educational skills in ways that stretch the concept of the professional self, the teacher has a choice. Some teachers give up, or allow the student to "choose to fail," or set up expectations that doom the student to defeat. Teachers of grace seek new methods. Teachers of grace try new ways to connect with the student and to connect the student with the learning. Teachers of grace remediate basic skills to allow for higher-level thinking. Teachers of grace demonstrate love for the Christ inside each student by drawing lines of acceptable behavior, remaining consistent, and setting goals that allow students to experience success.

The measurement of success warrants discussion from a Christian perspective in light of the concept of grace. While the Bible speaks often and unfavorably about judging others, the people following Jesus clearly recognized Christ as a teacher—albeit, not one who corrected with a red pen. The Bible does speak to accountability and integrity, fundamental components of assessment in education. Assessment can cause anxiety for many educators because the stakes are often high. In the lower grades, poor marks mean distressing conversations around the dinner table. In the secondary grades, poor marks can mean the difference between a first or second tier university. In higher education, grades on a transcript can determine admissions to graduate school—a heavy burden for any educator to carry.

Considering assessment as a means to shape student learning through a focus upon the knowledge and skills mastered allows the student a view of self that remains free from any personal judgment. When students understand expectation of performance and have multiple opportunities to meet performance objectives, assessment becomes a learning process whereby students see improvement. Even though most institutions require some sort of final mark for a transcript, the anxiety many educators face when converting formative evaluations to summative grades is lessened by the careful feedback provided earlier in the course. Some mask the anxiety of grades by the reliance upon an electronic grade book and student work reduced to numerical form. While a number provides little fodder for argument, and students understand how a number reflects progress in a course, a number does not provide clear explanations of the concepts mastered and skills honed in each course. A Christian educator takes seriously the need to assess with integrity, and integrity demands honest formative feedback that leads to student achievement rather than a few opportunities for students to produce evidence of memorization in a mid-term or final summative evaluation.

In short, teachers of grace never relinquish best practice in favor of personal convenience or comfort. Numbers are convenient and electronic grade books remove the subjective assessments of growth, whole group teaching and reliance upon lecture means less planning for individuals, rigid due dates and impossible expectations allow for positional power on the part of the teacher, but none of these practices adhere to either strong teaching practice or the ethical imperatives of the Christian educator. Numbers have a place in education as do the lecture and due dates; however, the Christian educator must find ways to combine rigor with practice that brings all students to high levels of mastery. A traditional view of education allows 10 percent in the mastery category. This inherently discriminatory view leaves 90 percent of the student body below the mark of mastery. Ninety percent of God's children receive less than 100 percent of course content? Think about it. Moving into a vision of education as providing the very best in learning to expand and magnify the potential of all students requires grace at the very core of teaching.

Discussion Questions

How do you demonstrate grace to difficult students?

Describe the characteristics of students who most need our grace.

Describe some educational practices that you
could adjust to better exemplify grace.

GRACE IN RELATIONSHIPS

Maximizing the promise within each student involves establishing appropriate relationships with students, parents and guardians, teachers and other school personnel, and with the larger community. An invitational classroom climate where learning takes precedence necessitates a trusting relationship between the students and the teacher, and the teacher and those important to the student. Numerous writers have addressed the issue of relationships in a learning context (Birch & Ladd, 1997; Pianta, 1999), but the idea of grace as a precursor to relationship leaves the Christian educator with much to consider. And grace and love are not always easy. Students may come into classrooms with poor attitudes about teachers and learning coupled with a history of failure. Students may come to us from homes where parents denigrate the educational system or perhaps fear what they perceive as positions of power; and thus, the teacher becomes the antagonist in the story of school. The plot is all so familiar with a predictable conclusion for both teacher and student—unless grace becomes a theme.

Concepts of love and acceptance form the foundation of relationships, and grace requires the presence of both. Christian love—the love-your-neighbor-as-yourself kind of love—brings teachers like Mrs. Callahan into relationship with students like Arthur, who was not always tremendously likeable. The acceptance of a unique individual, one who may not ascribe to our ideals of behavior and philosophy, along with Christian love will serve as a foundation for a grace-filled relationship. We know from developmental frameworks (Erickson, 1950; Vygotsky, 1978) that learning requires the sense of acceptance and belonging, and the embodiment of grace provides the portal into which we can begin developing relationships that lead to learning and also develop the heart and soul of another human being.

Not long into my teaching in higher education, I ran into my first real challenge to grace-filled teaching. A student, one many educators would describe without many words of compassion, became a tremendous challenge to my course planning, attitude about students, and ideals about a career in higher education. Incessantly negative, cynical, and sometimes quite rude, this student managed to push every button possible. When describing his behavior to a colleague, I mentioned that my past fourth graders had better self-regulation. That statement made me realize that even adult students entered my classroom with a need for grace and love, and this became a defining moment that mitigated feelings of frustration and annoyance. Teachers may not like every child, but they must love all children. As with a child, the decision to purposely demonstrate grace in the relationship with my adult student changed my attitude about him and my place in education. While this challenging person never developed into a student who brought joy to the classroom, the grace, rather like forgiveness, enabled me to move ahead and to find joy within my own act of teaching. This grace relies upon the pedagogy mentioned earlier, the acceptance of all students as worthy people created by God for unique purposes, and relationships that allow learning to remain a priority in the classroom.

What happens when our faith and value systems conflict with those of our students? Accepting that all students are created by God; and therefore, worthy of grace presents real challenges for some Christian educators. Our Christian worldview must dictate our actions, including the call to treat every student with justice and equality so that diverse viewpoints are included in the educational setting—even when they do not match our own. Several years ago, while still teaching undergraduates, I taught a class in multicultural education and within it sat a diverse group of students, even though at first glance they all appeared to represent the demographic of the rural community in which the college was situated. Upon closer inspection, I found, aside from the obvious few underrepresented cultures, students who lived with significant others, students who used controlled substances as recreation, students who had grown up in poverty, athletes, intellectuals, liberals, conservatives, one Wiccan, and two who identified as homosexual.

Thankfully, I quickly learned that homogeneity in a small rural private college is nothing more than a myth, and that reality surfaced once I looked deeply enough and past the obvious. My challenge was to shape this group into a community that honored each other for the gifts each brought to the classroom every Tuesday and Thursday. Instead of using my value system as a lens through which I viewed each individual, the recognition of the unique gifts of each individual served as the way in which I viewed my students. My students. The result was the building of relationships that have lasted until this very day. It also allowed me to understand how Jesus could love young people who do not adhere to customary Christian traditions. These students are His, too. The fundamental educational mandate requiring the creation of an invitational environment where all are honored and respected aligns directly with the Christian concept of grace. Jesus did not discriminate and dole out grace only to those who followed the prevailing cultural norm—quite the opposite, really. Inviting others in instead of pushing them out is grace in action and it allows for the formation of rewarding relationships.

Turnitin.com advertises as "the global leader in addressing plagiarism." A common practice in my neighborhood school district is to have high school students set up an account and submit all written work to Turnitin.com before submission. Ask any high school student why teachers use Trunitin.com and chances are you will likely get the following answer: "They don't trust us." Notice the distinct they–we division between teachers and students. No doubt, cheating and plagiarizing are immoral, but "guilty until proven innocent," the prevailing philosophy behind the choice to use the service, does little to promote either relationships or teaching about moral decisions, not to mention specific knowledge about the avoidance of plagiarism. Trusting students and then offering support when poor decisions are made is the foundation of discipline—discipleship in action. True discipline enacted out of love promotes a culture of *us*. Allowing students to fail, without letting them fail the course, provides an opportunity for both the teacher and student to learn. Trust, accompanied by the realization that we live in a broken world where people make the wrong choices, and forgiveness and grace prompt us to move forward and experience growth.

Many educators fear relationships, and establishing boundaries often becomes a topic of discussion in teacher preparation programs as well as within teachers' lounges across the country. The actions of a few troubled and unscrupulous individuals within our profession have left many educators fearful of "getting too close" to students, literally and figuratively, and the resulting perception on the part students are that teachers and professors do not care about them. Birch & Ladd (1997) and Pianta (1999) highlight the importance of learning in relationships and we have established fairly well the agreement that the student-teacher relationship profoundly affects learning. Healthy and appropriate relationships build confident and resilient learners. (See the Search Institute's website.) Entering into relationships with the purpose of building others—and an attitude of servant-hood—is good and right. The call to teach inherently includes the call to serve in relationship.

Fostering healthy relationships with students also requires flexibility briefly discussed earlier in the section on grace in pedagogy. In healthy student-educator relationships, flexibility becomes non-negotiable. When educators see each student as an individual with whom a relationship exists based on trust and support, rigid rules of operation can damage the learning process. Individuals have unique circumstances and no amount of planning when constructing a syllabus can prepare educators or students for what may come during the course.

My daughter, a student at a Christian university, told me that she accidently submitted an assignment to the wrong place in the electronic class site. She caught it early and informed the professor, requesting with an apology, that he send it back to her so she could re-submit in the proper location. From my vantage point as an educator who began teaching first graders and has moved up through the grades to the graduate level, it appeared as a reasonable request and a common error that has no bearing what so ever upon a student's demonstration of progress toward course goals, so what is the big deal? Apparently, for students in that course, it measures up there with the most egregious of offenses. In the same semester, my daughter neglected to transfer two answers on an exam from the test sheet to the answer sheet. The professor saw her omissions and gave her the points for the questions. Which professor will my daughter look to as a mentor, a fair and reasonable person, and as a worthy educator? The little graces in the form of flexibility and understanding go along way in establishing a climate where students want to do well for themselves and they want to do well for the professor because of the honor established within the relationship with that educator.

When educators honor students and demonstrate that through grace, students honor educators and reciprocate likewise. While grace-filled pedagogy asks for timely and thorough feedback, educators are also human with demands and obligations outside the academy. When a teacher has a solid relationship with the students, and life burdens steal time meant for reading student papers before the next class session, an honest explanation from the educator suffices and understanding abounds. Educators who do not have the relationships in place get poor evaluations, poor ratings on websites, and have students scheduling around their course times. Often, educators are reluctant to offer any flexibility or leeway to students because they fear adding to what they refer to as "student entitlement." Many educators see in students a "prerogative to demand" that they attempt to battle at any cost. Do some students demand? Absolutely. Are students entitled to a quality education from servant professors and teachers who honor each student as an individual with whom God has found favor? Absolutely. Our hearts hold the balance, not the syllabus or guidebook or policy manual. Responding in grace with the recognition of relationship and individual uniqueness suppresses any sense of entitlement one might find in a student.

Discussion Questions

When have you found yourself in conflict with a student?
How did you resolve the conflict?

When has classroom practice or policy conflicted
with your concept of grace?

Do you fear entering into relationships with students?

When your heart conflicts with practice, what do you do?

GRACE IN COLLEGIALITY

Gary Tiffin discusses at length the concept of community in a later chapter in this book. A strong connection exists between community, collaboration, and grace. In the current educational climate, collaboration with colleagues surrounding student achievement proliferates regardless of the type of school environment. Teaching, no longer a solitary act whereby one enters a classroom and closes the door to the outside world, now requires that we work as a team. Just as students learn in community and relationship, so do educators. While this cannot come as an earth shattering revelation, getting some educators to work collaboratively might just require something along the lines of an apocalyptic threat. After all, teachers have worked in crowded isolation for centuries. When teachers leave their congested classrooms and enter into collegial work, students realize amazing results because of the learning that takes place in community. Working in community toward an institutional goal, or individual student progress, allows the collective good and knowledge of the group to develop plans and solutions that rise above what one individual could accomplish. School districts around the world now grant time within a school day for teachers to collaborate. University professors are expected to serve on committees and it serves as a measure of worthiness in issues of tenure and promotion. Teamwork, like community described by Tiffin, leads to a stronger environment in which our students learn.

Collegiality, the sharing of responsibility between and among those working together toward a common goal, requires transparency and excellent communication. While we value collegiality and collaboration between educators, working with others brings its own challenges in the form of personality differences, communication styles, competiveness, and different passions. Working with others who are not like us can either challenge and inform for personal and group growth, or challenge and overwhelm leading to stagnation and a loss of opportunity to move forward. Only when the challenge accompanies grace, can we begin to grow together toward a common goal. Grace in collegial relationships takes on forgiveness and inclusive communication and it focuses on the common good of the organization as opposed to personal agendas.

Gone are the days of phone calls and letters to arrange meetings or to disseminate information. Email, social websites, and text messages have replaced many of the communication methods we have used for years. We are left with new ways to receive and send important material, which means we also have new ways to interpret the written word. Danger lurks not in the technology, but in the immediacy of the communication and in the decoding of any implied message. A grace filled collegial culture must include an agreement to communicate with honesty, transparency and grace. Professors, teachers, and institutions ought to consider how communication styles and content might affect students and families in everything from syllabi and report cards to invitations and general information. Collegial and grace-filled communication also includes the courage to say the difficult with that love-your-neighbor-as-yourself type of love. Withholding information that can lead to growth, ease job performance, or promote belonging and inclusion represents a separation from God's desires for his people. Knowledge is power and withholding knowledge represents a duplicitous undermining of the wellbeing of others—the opposition of grace.

Grace in collegial relationships also requires that we refrain from judgment based upon myopic philosophical perspectives. We learn from Matthew 7:1–5 that we must not judge, and yet Christian educators, accountable to God and to each other, might expect gentle confrontation if actions do not align with mission. The point remains that hypocrisy has no place in our schools, and colleagues who value each other see multiple ways to view each other's practice. For example, I have a colleague who when teaching undergraduates used to require all assignments to be turned in on time in order to avoid a grade penalty. He says he told students, "The trains run on time in England." He makes the point that students are accountable to the schedule and need to learn to manage time. On the other hand, I have always allowed extra time on assignments provided that what gets turned in represents quality work reflective of the extended due date. I understand that trains run on time in England, but I also understand that other trains arrive regularly. I want my students to find solutions. Time management verses problem-solving—both are valuable. I do not judge my colleague's practice as poor, inferior, or ineffective, as I am sure he would not judge mine as substandard or too lenient. We have different perspectives and different desires concerning our students. He has students who to this day (years later) come back with expressions of gratitude, as do I. Conversely, I do expect that this colleague would hold me accountable to upholding institutional mission and Christian living.

Christian living often excludes celebration of personal success lest it become boastful (see Romans 12:3). How do we gracefully celebrate the success of others? While some interpret the announcement of any success as boasting, against which the Bible warns repeatedly, educators have long understood the importance of building self-esteem in students by celebrating successes. Building the confidence of our students comes easily and most would agree that building the confidence of our colleagues also comes effortlessly as a joy and a privilege, but others adamantly disagree and feel the announcement of a professional accomplishment causes others to feel inferior. Recently, a colleague came into my office with a check for a substantial sum of money. When I asked her what it was for, she explained that she had written a grant and just received the funding. Joy was written all over her face, and I asked her if she was going to announce this at the department-wide meeting later that afternoon. Her reply was, "Oh, no, I couldn't possibly." I asked permission to announce the funding of the grant that allowed her to carry our ministry to people on another continent and that was acceptable, but she was not comfortable sharing this news with her colleagues assembled as a body of Christian educators. While there is a difference between *I am happy because this hard work paid off* and *I am better than you because this I accomplished,* many Christians do not acknowledge the nuanced variation in the two statements. Richard Graves tells us that grace transcends the ego and that it allows us to see ourselves universally (Foehr & Schiller, 1997). I suggest we seek ways to support each other and celebrate these happy moments in our lives as teachers and professors because they sustain us and allow us to continue to interact with each other in grace-filled ways that lead to the advancement of our field.

Promotion and tenure committees judge and assess professors upon their contributions in teaching, scholarship, and service. While elementary and secondary teachers might not have service requirements, I doubt many Christian educators spend long hours outside the classroom in idle wandering. Rather, most might have trouble honoring the Sabbath due to an over-commitment to serve in various roles in and out of the school. We received grace through the ultimate sacrifice, and many Christians, in turn, sacrifice time and resources in order that they might extend grace to others. Serving others and doing for the least of these through the use of our hands and feet as agents of Christ set Christians apart from non-Christian colleagues. While non-Christians might very well serve others in important and meaningful ways clocking in more volunteer hours than what might seem humanly possible, the recognition that we serve out of a commitment to Jesus, and in recognition of His grace, adds a dimension to the service that can complicate. University-wide volunteer days, church stewardship committees, Saturdays with Habitat for Humanity, and teaching Sunday School all look good on resumes but carry no more value in the eyes of the Lord than sitting with a colleague editing a paper, working with a teaching partner to assemble a bulletin board, or acting as a sounding board for a colleague contemplating a career move. Graceful service is quiet and has the interest of another at heart.

Grace in collegiality requires an assessment of aptitude of self and others, and an acknowledgment of gifts and areas for improvement. If our colleagues have communicated with grace, we have an understanding of our gifts and challenges as perceived by others. An unemotional assessment of this knowledge leads us to personal growth and allows us to use gifts to help others through service. Because gifts are God given, the use of gifts to promote and assist others demonstrates graceful living.

Discussion Questions

When has your grace been challenged in a collegial relationship?

In what ways do you extend grace to your colleagues?

How can a grace-filled relationship with a colleague
affect student achievement?

GRACE IN SCHOLARSHIP

God's grace gives us unique gifts. Through the act of scholarship, we use the gifts to advance our field and the practice of others. Literature exists that speaks directly to the challenges of Christian scholars (Craig & Gould, 2007; Hughes, 2005; Marsden, 1997) and while scholarship can emerge from Christians serving in secular institutions as well as from those in Christian institutions, the nature of the scholarship reflects God's purpose and grace. Seeking new knowledge honors God, as God provides the source of all truth. Our work as Christian scholars, particularly those within the sciences and social sciences, can lead to disequilibrium, but then Jesus asked his disciples to think in different ways. Scholarship that seeks truth, regardless of what that scholarly inquiry reveals, ultimately leads back to God as the source of all creation and the model of grace. The interaction between a dynamic field and a consistent God encourages spirited discussion within classrooms and among colleagues, and it encourages scholarship that promotes faith for faculty and students alike. Scholarship motivated by fascination and a desire to serve and advance our field while promoting students and colleagues satisfies the godly qualities of wonder and grace.

Educators exemplify grace in scholarship by upholding standards and giving researchers respectful consideration. That almost sounds paradoxical. Producing good work, helping those under our tutelage rise to accepted standards of scholarship, and holding ourselves accountable to our colleagues upholds the ideals of our profession. At the same time, when we encounter scholarship, we should assume the researcher has given his or her best effort to expand the field; and therefore, allow us to appraise the work based upon how it informs our discipline rather than our personal preferences. Disagreement about research or scholarship must remain within the context of the work rather than moving into the realm of relationship, and at the same time, we must recognize any bias. Many educators struggle with providing feedback that students or colleagues might perceive as negative, but when the feedback provides opportunities for growth, we have a professional and ethical obligation to correct, mentor and guide those who have not met expected criteria.

The complex relationship between epistemology, content knowledge, instructional strategies, and scholarship informs the way Christian educators choose to infuse faith into the learning experience for students. The timeworn integration language used by scholars in the Christian education arena (Badley, 1994; Hasker, 1992) leave some seeking ways to simplify, glorify, and personalize the infusion of faith into teaching and learning experiences. Using faith as a filter from which we view instructional choices and course content in relationship to student need and present culture allows educators to speak of faith infusion in ways that remain relevant and meaningful. Furthermore, grace in scholarship seeks ways to promote meaningful discourse and discovery while at the same time advancing the university, aiding other scholars, and motivating the productivity of the researcher. The attempted infusion of faith into scholarship, learning experiences, or interactions with colleagues that does not include an intentional awareness of God's sustaining grace may superficially satisfy the requirements of a faith-based institution, but an attempt to call upon and impart God's grace reflects and magnifies Him in powerful ways that can influence others in ways we could not do left to our own resources.

Ernest Boyer (1990) regards teaching as scholarship and recognizes the commitment needed to stay current in the field by reading widely in addition to planning that considers solid pedagogical methods. Glassick, Huber, and Maeroff (1997) advance Boyer's assertions and say that scholarly teaching brings the ideals of the academy to the student and thus prepares them to enter therein primed and ready to reciprocate through the promotion of the scholarship of others. Regarding teaching as scholarship accentuates the significance of educators' work in the shaping of students. When grace enters teaching, students experience the best educators have to offer; gain skills, knowledge and a deeper faith; then leave with the skills and dispositions to offer grace to others.

Discussion Questions

How have you been challenged by scholarship in your field?

In what ways do you advance your field?

What other ways to you see a connection between
grace and scholarship?

CONCLUSION

We have come full circle. Grace in the way we choose to teach, in our relationships with students and colleagues, and in our scholarship reflects
the essence of exemplary education. As recipients of the unearned gift of
grace, we must accept it with deep gratitude and we then become agents of
grace passing it on to our students. Incorporating the concept of grace into
the work of educators leads to transformational teaching in which students
learn not only content, but the values of the academy, how educators extend
God's love, and how they can reciprocate the gift of grace in their own lives.

REFERENCES

Badley, K. (1994). The faith/learning integration movement in Christian higher education: Slogan or substance? *Journal of Research on Christian Education*, 3(1), 13–33.

Birch, S. H., & Ladd, G. W. (1997). The teacher-child relationship and children's early school adjustment. *Journal of School Psychology*, 35, 61–79.

Boyer, E. L. (1990). *Scholarship reconsidered: Priorities of the professoriate*. San Francisco: Jossey-Bass and The Carnegie Foundation for the Advancement of Teaching.

Craig, W. L., & Gould, P. M. (Eds.). (2007). *The two tasks of the Christian scholar: Redeeming the soul, redeeming the mind*. Wheaton, IL: Crossway.

Erickson, E. (1950). *Childhood and society*. New York: Norton.

Foehr, R. P., & Schiller, S. A. (Eds.). (1997). *The spiritual side of writing: Releasing the learner's whole potential*. Portsmouth, NH: Boynton/Cook.

Glassick, C. E., Huber, M. T., & Maeroff, G. I. (1997). *Scholarship assessed: Evaluation of the professoriate*. San Francisco: Jossey-Bass and The Carnegie Foundation for the Advancement of Teaching.

Hasker, W. (1992). Faith-learning integration: An overview. *Christian Scholar's Review*, 21(3), 234–248.

Hughes, R. T. (2005). *The vocation of a Christian scholar: How Christian faith can sustain the life of the mind*. Grand Rapids: Eerdmans.

Marsden, G. M. (1997). *The outrageous idea of Christian scholarship*. New York: Oxford University Press.

Muehl, W. (1995). *The Living Pulpit* (January–March).

Pianta, R. C., (1999). *Enhancing relationships between children and teachers*. Washington, DC: American Psychological Association.

Tomlinson, C. A. (1999). *The differentiated classroom: Responding to the needs of all learners*. Alexandria, VA: ASCD.

Vygotsky, L. S. (1978). *Mind and society: The development of higher psychological processes*. Cambridge: Harvard University Press.

http://www.search-institute.org/developmental-assets.

https://turnitin.com/static/index.php.

2

Joy

GINNY D. BIRKY

THINKING ABOUT JOY TAKES me back to my Sunday School classroom as a child. Hymns and choruses often speak of the joy we experience as Christians. Before I started writing this chapter on joy, and particularly as it relates to teaching, I had no idea there were so many books, chapters, articles, and blogs on the subject. I was overwhelmed with how broad the topic was. At the same time, I was also chagrined to realize how little I think about joy in relation to my teaching. The thoughts that follow reflect my exploration into the topic of joy: What is it? Do I have it? Where does it come from? How do I obtain and nourish it? And lastly, how do I apply it with my students and in my classroom?

Students in my fourth period high school classroom entered my class as they normally do that fall day. The lesson was on the emotional development of children. Knowing that it is helpful for students to connect their past experiences with new learning, I asked them for examples of positive or negative childhood experiences they had that could affect them as teenagers and in their adult lives. The room was quiet for only five seconds. But then Darin raised his hand and proceeded to tell about the time his dad left the family when he was seven, and how he still wonders if he personally had anything to do with his dad's disappearance. I was surprised that someone would share something so personal that quickly. Soon Amber shared about the time their house burned to the ground. She said she often worried about waking up at night to another burning house, and this time losing her family members. As the third student was sharing a story about the physical abuse he (yes, he) had experienced, he started to cry. Soon another student spoke up and was crying. I got up to pass around a box of tissues and wondered to myself what I had done to prompt this many students to share so deeply with emotions unchecked. I remember questioning in my mind if this was acceptable, whether I had stepped over the line, and what I should do now to stop the personal stories. Before it was over, eight students had shared their stories and almost everyone was crying, either with quiet tears, or sobbing. Students got up and went to put their arms around their friends to comfort them. When the bell rang for lunch, most of them stayed to talk and pull themselves together before leaving the room. For days, these students were in my prayers in ways they had never been before. I will never forget this day!

Why do I share a sad story in a chapter on joy? What is the connection? A story about my classroom that appears to be painful also prompts me to consider how I find joy in the midst of this experience. What I know from research and personal stories is that one of the sources of joy for teachers is when they feel satisfaction and meaning in their role as teacher. I don't know why, but I went home that day with the satisfaction that I had made a difference in the lives of some of my students. That satisfaction gave my job meaning. To this day, even though this happened fifteen years ago, it remains one of the most rewarding days of my teaching career. Blessed Columba Marmion, a writer and beatified Catholic spiritual director, stated that "joy is the echo of God's life in us!" (Ball, 2001, p. 11). I can only believe that I echoed God's life in my classroom that day as well. That alone turns my satisfaction into joy!

WHY JOY?

Like all good things in life, the Bible recommends joy! Ecclesiastes 8:15 says, "So I commend the enjoyment of life, because nothing is better for a man under the sun than to . . . be glad. Then joy will accompany him in his work all the days of the life God has given him . . ." Other translations use similar phrases: "I commend joy" (English Standard), "I recommend having fun" (NLT), and "I commend pleasure" (American Standard). Jesus also intended that our lives be happy and joyful, rather than weighed down with burdens, boredom, and sadness.

A sense of joy and engagement is important for both teachers and students. However, it is an especially hard time for the field of education. We are faced with large class sizes, budget cuts, pressure to produce high test scores, the need to satisfy parents, and the desire to prepare students for life. In the introduction to his book, *Stories of the Courage to Teach: Honoring the Teacher's Heart*, Intrator (2002) describes teachers as feeling underappreciated, undermined, overwhelmed, isolated, and vulnerable (which is the reason he calls for the renewal of a teacher's heart). It's easy for a teacher to be concerned, criticize, and complain because we have many reasons to feel more stress than joy.

But without experiencing joy myself, work will eat me up and I won't be an effective teacher or colleague. If I don't bring joy to my classroom or to my students, I doubt if they will truly engage, take risks, laugh, and have fun.

DEFINING JOY

So what is this joy that I should feel and possess? What is this joy that I so desire? What about happiness? I know that being happy and joyful are two different things, but are they related, and if so, how?

Happiness versus Joy

The pursuit of happiness seems to be an instinctive drive for human beings. People seek it in varying ways and intensities (Ritenbaugh, 1998). We tend to use the word "happy" more than "joy," at least in a secular sense. We say "I'm so glad (happy) my students did well on that test" instead of "I feel so much joy when I realize how well my students did on that test." Webster defines joy as the emotion evoked by well-being or success, the state of happiness, and the source or cause of delight (Merriam-Webster online). *Webster's New World Dictionary* defines joy as synonymous with words such as happy, glad, and cheerful. A thesaurus relates it to delight, contentment, satisfaction, and pleasure. But as Ritenbaugh (1998) points out, these definitions do not consider the causes of joy, how it is expressed, or how long it lasts.

Biblical Joy

The concept of joy is a major theme in the Bible; words such as joy, joyfulness, and rejoicing are used over 400 times (Collins, 1998). However, Ford (1998) said that when the early church began experiencing hardships and persecution, the word joy was tied to trials and suffering. In the same way, sometimes I feel the weight of what's going on in the educational system. When that happens, I identify more with the trials than the rewards. But I must persevere for the sake of my students as well as myself. Hebrews 12:1–2 says "let us run with perseverance the race marked out for us. Let us fix our eyes on Jesus the author and perfecter of our faith, who for the joy set before him endured the cross, scorning its shame . . ." Sometimes in the classroom at the end of the day I don't know if I have made a difference, but I've persevered through it because of the hope that it would lead to the learning and joy that would follow. I know I have the joy of eternal life awaiting me. And in the classroom I also have the rewards of a daily job well done.

True joy is a "cheerful peace of mind . . ." (Ford, 1998, p. 5). It is not something that exists in our head or heart, but instead it is the Holy Spirit working in us (Ritenbaugh, 1998). A friend described joy in the exact same way. She said "Joy for me is when the sun shines, . . . when I don't have so much stress that my body aches from the tension, . . . when I look into my husband's eyes, . . . when I experience my smallness in the middle of God's grand creation, and when I rest" (email 5/18/11).

I wonder how often I feel real joy. I frequently sense happiness, satisfaction, contentment, and pleasure. But I've asked myself how often I feel true joy—that delight, gratitude, and peace that only comes from God, and that makes me glad I am alive. How often do I feel the calmness and resting that seems evident in my colleague's description of joy? I've been thinking a lot about that. She said she experiences joy when she "rests." Perhaps that is why my joy is not always full. If I am rushing, I may experience happiness, but it doesn't have a chance to move from there to joy. It is hard to rest. It is hard to slow down in life and in the classroom in order to provide space and stillness. But I once again commit to resting with the hope of experiencing the fullness of joy.

Joy is a Fruit of the Spirit

Collins (1998) stated in his article that joy is more than an emotion; it is a "quality . . . that should characterize our lives as Christians" (p. 2). Maybe that's why it is one of the fruits of the spirit. Galatians 5:22–23 lists nine visible attributes of a Christian's life; joy is the second on the list. Because of its high priority, perhaps it should be given more attention in our daily living if we want to bear good fruit. Joy is like edible fruit on a vine; it is a byproduct of our lives and something we must cultivate and nourish if we want to bear excellent fruit.

Ford (1998) said joy is knowing that God has worked with us (pruned us) to become more like him. It's an "awareness that we survived and we grew" (p. 5). In the classroom, I have questioned how I responded to a challenging student or colleague, whether I planned the most effective strategy to teach lesson content, or why I got an angry email from a parent. I feel strongly that reflection and self-evaluation should be a continual practice for teachers. But I sometimes fail. And when I do, I can either see myself as a poor teacher, or I can see it as God's way to make me more like Him. Bearing fruit then, is a part of God's workmanship in me. I experience joy not only when I am being "pruned," but also when I see the fruit of my labors in the classroom, when students are learning, happy, confident, and safe. As a Christian, I recognize that Christ is the one helping me bring forth fruit.

Discussion Questions

How would you define and describe joy?

Do you have true joy, or is it mostly happiness?

What would your students say about your joy?

SOURCES OF JOY

In the Scriptures we are told that Jesus is the true source of our joy. For example, "the joy of the LORD is your strength" (Nehemiah 8:10). And, "God gives wisdom, knowledge, and joy to those who please him" (Ecclesiastes 2:26, NLT). Joy only comes with God's presence in our lives, knowing that he has been with us in the past, is with us now, and will be in the future. With that knowledge and confidence comes true joy!

While joy may be a spiritual practice that I must cultivate, it should not be something I seek, nor is it an end in itself. Instead it is a blessing from God that I receive as a gift and that I can experience. I want this blessing both inside and outside of my classroom. While the only real source of joy is from God, there are numerous ways we sense and experience that joy in our everyday lives.

Vocation: A Calling

Many Christians call teaching a "calling" or a vocation rather than a job or an occupation. But I don't know what that means for those of our teacher/professor colleagues who are wonderful teachers but not believers. I personally chose to be a teacher when I was in elementary school, and I continued on that path until I became one. I never wanted to do anything else. But in those early years, I wanted to be a teacher more for reasons of self-interest and ego rather than one of serving God. As a teacher-educator now, sometimes our candidates take on a "saving and helping" mentality. They want to be teachers because they want to make things better, make a difference, convey their love of a subject, or save the world! Sam Intrator (2002) shares this same sentiment when he reflects on his first teaching job:

> I vividly remember walking out the door after my first day as a teacher at Sheepshead Bay High School in Brooklyn. I was twenty-one years old, and as I walked down the street, passing children playing ball, high schoolers waiting for the bus, and seniors lugging groceries home, I felt so worthy and important. I was a teacher, and this was important work. It was electrifying, and I'll not soon forget the raw jolt of earnestness and responsibility that came with the realization that I had my own classroom and that 180 young people would look to me for direction, support, and guidance. (p. xxxvi)

This idealism and these desires are understandable and honorable. But I now believe that a deeper sense of calling, sometimes not identified as such, is what keeps us in the profession. Without it, most of us would either have left the job, or been miserable in continuing.

Intrator (2002) cited the result of numerous surveys that revealed why teachers came to the profession. These participants believed they could play a "thoughtful, caring, and influential role in the lives of young people" (p. xxxvii). He calls this motivation to teach "for reasons of the heart" (p. 4). These reasons included a love for children and a satisfaction in watching them grow, the realization that children and youth bring out the best in them, and because they have hope in making the world a better place (Ayers, as cited in Intrator, p. xxxvii).

Parker Palmer (2007) believes that this sense of call and giftedness for teaching goes beyond a vocation. He explained it as the intersection between the "inner self and the outer world" (p. 31). Palmer stated that no matter how much our vocation is valued by others, it is a violation of ourselves if we do it for the wrong reasons. And when we do something that does not flow from within our identity, we also violate others with whom we are in contact, our colleagues and our students.

I wonder, then, if joy can only result when one chooses teaching for the right reasons. Ritenbaugh (1998) said, "Joy is the sign that life has found its purpose" (p. 6). I sense I have found my purpose when my teacher candidates come to the realization that they have chosen the right profession. It brings me joy because I feel I have had an influence in that affirmation. The following three examples are from emails sent to me by teacher candidates when they realized they had made the right choice to become a teacher:

- Thanks for everything again! You helped me rediscover why I decided to become a teacher, which is to help people and inspire young people. Thanks again, and I am forever grateful.

- [In the first 4 months of this program], I rediscovered . . . the joy of learning. For a long time, I had been in a rut and disengaged from many opportunities to grow. I hope to leverage this awareness and connect with my [future] students through it.

- [In this program], I had a great experience and feel I am ready to go teach.

When I read or hear comments such as the ones above, not only do I feel joy, but I believe the students writing these statements also felt joy. Ritenbaugh (1998) said it well: "When a person feels good about life, about who and what he is, what he is doing with his life and where it is headed, a sense of joy is always present" (p. 7).

Because I believe Jesus has called me to live my life for Him, I assume I could feel fulfilled in other vocations as well. In my forty years as a teacher and college professor, there were two times when I actually thought about doing something else. The notion was strong enough that I remember looking at the want ads to see what else I might do. In neither case was I considering a change because I didn't like what I was doing. I love what I do and gain great satisfaction from it. Instead, those feelings were a result of wondering how long I was willing to work so many hours in a week, including nights, weekends, and vacations. I'm still "here," still teaching, and still enjoying it. I know part of the reason I am still teaching is because of the joy I feel as a result of the work I do.

Relationships

Relating to students is the ultimate connection and source of satisfaction in teaching. Principals tell us that the main quality they look for in a teacher candidate is whether or not they like and talk about kids. High school teachers sometime find it easier to love their content first and then their students. Both are important, but we don't teach content, we teach students.

In a keynote address on where he finds joy in teaching, Johnson (2003) explained, "Most of my time [at school] is in one way or another dedicated to teaching. I do go to committee meetings and I do have to grade, but in between all of that stuff I get to go to class" (p. 2). How wonderful to always see going to class as something I "get to do" instead of something I "have to do." There is something about the privilege of going to class that has the possibility of bringing joy to both students and teacher.

I have had some wonderful colleagues over the years. In one of Jamaica's secondary schools in the early 1970s, my eyes were opened to diversity of culture and race. The staff room was a beautiful mix of Jamaican teachers who welcomed us to their island, and expatriate teachers who came from many countries around the world to teach. Because many of us were far away from home, the camaraderie we experienced created a lasting memory. In northeastern Ohio later in the 1970s, Elsie and I car-pooled to school, talking "school business" all the way to and from our jobs. In southwestern Colorado in the 1980s, Karen and I shared many department responsibilities, as well as hobbies and interests. At my Oregon high school in the 1990s, I took on new teacher leadership roles, was mentored by my principal, and enjoyed a sense of well-being in my career.

And now in my university position, I can honestly say it's the best of everything! I experience community each and every day with fellow believers and professionals. These colleagues are my friends, prayer partners, teachers, teammates, and fellow writers. We laugh, cry, pray, drive, and teach together! I love the physical hugs as well as the virtual ones at the end of an email. I enjoy the humor and the smiley faces that go into emails and texts. These colleagues teach me much. During times of feeling inadequate, I remember their affirmations. I am blessed beyond measure . . . and the result is joy! I agree with Daniels and Bizar (2005) when they say the work is easier and that joy is the outcome when we do important work with a group of people we know and love.

Satisfaction

I've frequently felt a sense of satisfaction in my role as teacher. The satisfaction comes from the belief that I've done a good job, that I've touched lives, and that I've made a difference—the exact same reasons we go into the teaching profession, as was discussed in the previous section.

In my doctoral research on teacher leadership (Birky, 2001), my goal was to determine where teacher leaders in secondary schools found meaning in their teacher leadership activities, given that they spent a lot of time and energy on tasks for which they were not compensated. I discovered that the main theme was satisfaction, indicating that my teacher leader participants found meaning in their activities because of the satisfaction they derived from their involvement as a teacher leader. They frequently used the word "enjoy" as they discussed satisfaction in their involvement and work. The teacher leaders in this study cited several ways this satisfaction played out in their lives: (1) Enjoyment—for example, one said, "I fundamentally enjoy what I do." They talked about having fun, loving their content area, and the ability to give up some leisure time because they genuinely found joy in their work. (2) Rewards with students—"I really like my students." Participants in the study commented that much of their satisfaction and reward came from helping their students achieve success. One said, "For me the meaning and reward comes in not . . . the day to day teaching . . . but it's those few and rare occasions when you get a student coming back and saying, 'Wow, you know, you did help, you made a difference.'" (3) Colleagues—they often spoke about the wonderful people with whom they worked. They described feelings of mutual admiration, the importance of teamwork, collaboration, and affirmation from their colleagues, both fellow teachers and administrators. In addition teacher leaders stated their satisfaction also came from the work they did with curriculum, and the stimulation and challenge their efforts provided.

In his book on *The Joy of Teaching* (2010), Hazel found similar comments when he talked to over 100 American and Canadian teachers about their work. He reminded his readers that one of the main roles of a teacher is to motivate students. But he wondered what teachers would say when asked what motivated them. Not surprisingly he found that the main source of motivation was the impact they have on students. A typical comment came from a middle school teacher in Calgary. She said, "Teaching is a joy because I like what I do" (p. 10). I've personally struggled with the "duh" in these statements about satisfaction. Is there anything more profound to give us satisfaction and joy? It doesn't seem so. Finding meaning and touching lives are the major reasons to teach.

I've wondered whether the satisfaction that leads to joy isn't also a result of Maslow's self-actualization. When I am confident I am meeting my potential and making full use of my skills and my talents, I feel satisfied, and therefore joyful.

Learning

I especially experience joy when my students learn what I've intended them to learn. "Ginny," Chuck wrote in an email, "after today's assessment workshop, and everything we've been going over in our classes, some new things are clicking. It is very exciting. I thank God for the opportunity to grow in this way, and for your guidance. As my cohort leader, I thought you'd like to hear this" (Chuck email, 10/7/09). Well yes, Chuck, I absolutely do want to hear this! Knowing that my students are learning keeps me going, and it brings me great joy. Hazel (2010) said, "Most educators find that their main source of joy is to take students at one level of learning and then to advance them as far as possible during the time they're together in the classroom or lab . . . satisfied teachers focus on students. They teach people—not reading, speech or economics" (p. 5).

For some students, learning comes more easily than for others. But a teacher's job is to help each child or student learn, whatever it takes to accomplish the task. When a student with whom we've worked long and hard shows evidence of learning, it seems like a miracle, and we are thankful. In reference to miracles, Psalm 28:7 says, "My hearts leaps for joy and I will give thanks to him in song."

Discussion Questions

What are your main sources of joy?

How were you "called" into this profession?

What are your greatest moments of joy in the classroom? Why?

LIVING AND PRACTICING JOY

Jesus intended for my life to overflow with joy. He said, "I have told you this so that my joy may be in you and that your joy may be complete" (John 15:11). But talking about joy and living it out in practice may be two different things. Joy comes easily in theory. I enjoy reading about it in the Bible and elsewhere. It is a gift, and who doesn't like gifts? But when it comes to applying the theory, well, it may be a different story. But instead of letting the reality of day-to-day routines and responsibilities hijack my joy, I want to consider ways I can live into the joy and have life to the fullest. I am a role model and among other great qualities, I want to model joy. By turning negative situations into something positive, forgiving myself, and having a thankful spirit, I at least move in the direction of joy. Then as I cultivate it in my life, I believe it will bear the fruit of joy.

Challenging Days and Challenging Students

In the introduction of Parker Palmer's (2007) book *The Courage to Teach*, he states that the book is written for "teachers who have good days and bad, and whose bad days bring the suffering that comes only from something one loves. It is for teachers who refuse to harden their hearts because they love learners, learning, and the teaching life" (p. 2).

I read a wonderful success story on turning a bad school day into a good day. On the Responsive Classroom website, Margaret Berry Wilson (2010) wrote an article on the importance of joy. One of the comments submitted after reading her article was by Rose, a third-grade teacher who said she had been getting weary of helping her students prepare for the upcoming testing days. She was tired of teaching test-taking strategies and giving numerous practice tests. Rose continued,

What an effective way to suck the joy out of the room. Well, it rained on Wednesday. When I say it rained, I mean it was a real toad-floater! In fact it rained so much that the worms . . . were scattered pitifully across all the sidewalks and parking lots. Our first grade buddies, who were studying worms, asked if we would come help save the worms by placing them in the dry soil under the roofline. Of course, we said yes and that was the start of the most joyful day of learning we've had in a long time. After the worm rescue, we returned to our room to talk about our adventure. We organized the events of the day onto cartoon strips, writing from the perspective of the worm. We wrote interesting "hook" sentences, added details and talked about how to create really great paragraphs using the cartoon strips as an organizer. We read finished paragraphs to our buddies. They read worm books to us. Spontaneously helping our little buddies by saving the worms brought joy and real learning into our classroom that day. I promised myself to continue to look daily for more opportunities for authentic reasons to read, write, share and care. (Berry, 2010)

With its multitude of seemingly unsolvable problems, sometimes the classroom is not a place of joy. Latisha complains about how Andy bothers her. Cameron argues about his grade. Five students did not turn in an exit slip on a day when I needed to assess student learning. Kasim has been tardy three days in a row and it is time to provide a consequence. And Jenn leaves the room in tears because she is worried about her dad losing his job. When Palmer (2007) asked teachers to name the biggest obstacle to good teaching, the most common answer was "my students." Some said their students were silent, others were withdrawn, some weren't able to carry on a conversation, and others had short attention spans. My graduate students tend to blame any kind of student challenge on either societal or family problems. I've told them, "You get what you get. Don't let it ruin your joy."

When we speak of joy, we often pair it with its counterparts: joy and sorrow, happiness and sadness, and smiles and tears. When we experience one, it increases our awareness of the other one. If we experience great joy from a relationship, when it is gone we feel the loss much more intensely (Spiritual Practices: Joy). Thus, in a classroom, I can be thankful for my feelings of inadequacy and sorrow, knowing that my fears and tears can be stepping stones to joy. Psalm 30:5 tells me that my weeping is temporary and that joy comes in the morning.

The Apostle Paul said to "consider [your trials] pure joy" (James 1:2). Negative experiences can be turned into something positive and help us grow. They can also change our perspective and our classrooms, as it did for Jessica when she had an experience that helped change her outlook on a past negative experience. In 2009, Jessica was a twenty-six year old graduate student in our teacher education program. She was the mother of a ten-year-old daughter and had spent five years in the business world in her first career. One Friday in February, two months before graduation, our students participated in a three-hour professional development workshop with a nationally known guest speaker. Dr. Donna Beegle grew up in generational poverty and told her dynamic story with great credibility and eloquence. Every story she shared was followed with insight for her audience of future educators so they could learn what worked and didn't work in the classrooms she attended as a child. During a break, I noticed Jessica had been crying. When I asked her if she wanted to talk, she said she did. The two of us went into a nearby room alone and she cried as she shared her heart. "That's my story," she said with tears streaming down her cheeks. "I can identify with everything she [Dr. Beegle] is saying. I grew up in poverty too. I had a child as a teenager for the same reason she did. I had those same feelings of shame about being poor and having brothers in jail. It's my story. I've always been so ashamed of it and didn't want anyone to know. But now I feel free to share it because it is me! And I can make a difference if I share it too." Jessica went on to say that when she came into the program she was torn in many directions. But in the two months before this date, she had been seeing a purpose for her life and felt it was aligning with God's purpose for her. We cried together, and then I prayed for her before rejoining the larger group. When I saw her later that day, I asked her if she was okay. She emphatically said, "Yes, I'm fine now!"

I once heard someone say, "On my worst day, someone is joyful. On my best day, someone is sad." Praise is seeing the larger perspective. Whether my day is a good one or not so good, I can always try to find the best in it, which will ideally influence my students to be joyful as well. I say "ideally" because what if it doesn't? I must then remember that joy is not a result of being happy or of everything going well. Instead, it is much deeper, more genuine, and more long lasting. So can I give myself permission to not be happy, to be disappointed, and sad? Yes, but since it comes from God, I will still want to cultivate joy in the midst of that sadness.

Forgiving Ourselves

Parker Palmer (2007) tells about a time he walked into his college classroom to begin his thirtieth year of teaching. He was happy to again be standing in front of students in a way that "engages my soul as much as any work I know. But I came home that evening convinced once again that I will never master this baffling vocation" (p. 9). Palmer was annoyed with some of his students—some talked too much and others not enough. He was also embarrassed by his own mistakes, and wondered if he should do something different than teach. I take great comfort in Palmer's transparency. I too have found myself dwelling on what I consider to be a mistake I made in my classroom, or for saying something that would have been better left unsaid or done differently. When I taught at the high school level, I occasionally regretted the way I handled a classroom management challenge. Now at the graduate level, I deal with different concerns. I recently made a poor choice of how to teach a particular topic to my graduate students. I used an idea I got from one of my colleagues who had done her graduate work on the topic. It might have worked for her but it didn't work for me! The self-assessments students completed at the end of the four-hour class reflected minimal understanding of the concept. I thought of this "failure" at least 20 times in the next three or four days, beating myself up each time, but also worrying that my students would see me in a negative light. I was finally able to let it go and to realize that I could grow from the experience if I wanted to—the choice was mine. Overcoming negative experiences doesn't come naturally, but when we do overcome, the result can be joy.

Spirit of Thankfulness

I am extremely thankful for wonderful teachers in my life. I feel joy just thinking about some of the most influential teachers I have had. They not only influenced me to become a teacher, but they also taught me how to live life to the fullest. For example:

- My mother, a capable, confident, and determined woman modeled how to get things done, and do them well.

- My father, a gentle and loyal man to whom I loved to ask questions of how and why, and in turn loved to answer my questions!

- My parents were my first teachers, and they taught and modeled Christian values.

- My younger sister allowed me to "teach" her in the hallway of our house. At one and one-half years my junior, she had no choice but to listen to me tell her all about life as if I really knew what I was talking about!

- Martha taught me how to play the piano and gain a skill that I later shared with many people in the churches in which I was involved.

- Mim Friesen was the teacher that inspired me to teach at the high school level (instead of Kindergarten, which was my original intent).

- Olive Wyse, a stoic college professor, taught me and challenged me to be professional.

- Don Francisco taught me that the message of Jesus did not have to be glitzy.

- John Steinbeck taught me that simple words can create powerful images.

- John DeBois, the last high school principal for whom I worked, taught me management skills, and encouraged and fostered teacher leadership qualities in me.

- George Copa modeled the qualities of a good college professor and gave me a passion for high school reform.

- Grace Balwit and Donna Phillips taught me how to be a faculty member in MAT.

- My husband Karl teaches me through all the books he reads and consistently makes me feel loved and accepted for who I am.

All my teachers had one thing in common—they all made me want to learn more. And I am a teacher who is a result of a combination of all of them. I love the words of Johnson (2003) when he said:

> A teacher can help you form a lens through which to view the world and can give you the tools to change that same world. A teacher gets to witness learning, confusions, comprehension, frustration, change, passion, and awareness—the very things that seem to be at the core of our humanity. In my life, my teachers have

made me want to be them—they have made the teaching process so alive that I wanted to teach . . . I want to be some conglomerate of Mr. Marshall and Michael Broide and Mr. Kenyon and Karyn Johnston and Brad Carroll. I don't teach because I want to give something back or because I have some altruistic goal of making the world a better place; I teach because it makes me feel alive. It is the person that I, completely selfishly, want to be. (p. 3)

Discussion Questions

When is the last time you deliberately turned something very negative into something positive?

Are you able to forgive yourself? If not, how might it be affecting you or your relationships?

Identify a teacher who you could thank for making a big difference in your own learning.

FOSTERING AN ENVIRONMENT WHERE JOY MAY EMERGE: NURTURING JOY IN THE CLASSROOM

I'm not sure I can create joy in my classroom. But I have ideas on how I can establish places and spaces that might help it emerge and grow. What does joy look like and feel like in a classroom? This is where the rubber meets the road, the application of all the theory and the Bible verses I've cited. The most challenging question, if not the most important one is: If Jesus were a student in my classroom, would He feel joy as a result of being there? Let's explore how the following might contribute to an environment where joy is nourished: attitude, justice, laughter/humor, teacher effectiveness, and engaging the soul.

Attitude

A young friend of mine spent a semester in Uganda as part of her college program. While there, she wrote an article for the church newsletter. Her testimony was one where she saw the negative side of her situation, but at the same time, also emphasized the positive. She said:

> I struggled with personal materialism as I witnessed poverty and constantly got frustrated from miscommunications with my host family. But, though life in Uganda was filled with uncomfortable and unpredictable lessons, I had an absolutely wonderful time, and God constantly gave me joy. I loved the sunny sky, my host sisters, conversations with a local shopkeeper, juicy fresh pineapple, rafting the Nile, and tea time with Ugandan students on campus. (Melissa, *Your NFC*, 2011)

Melissa's attitude shows that we may too easily take for granted the simple things that bring joy. In Gary Kilburg's chapter on Caring, he also reminds us that our attitude is a choice, and that we can only be the person God wants us to be when we model our lives after Him.

Ann Ball (2001) tells the story of a Salesian saint who spent his life working for the poor. He developed cancer and was nearing the end of his life. The doctors advised him to stay in bed, but he insisted on being with people and continuing to give service to others. "Since my sickness cannot be cured, why should I waste the rest of my life?" he asked. I've told my students that one of their greatest assets in the teacher education program and their job in schools is to have a positive attitude. Making the best of a negative situation is a challenge and even a discipline. What are the most negative situations in your classroom? Are you tired of NCLB influences? Are you ready for a year with fewer students for whom English is not their first language? Is the recess duty in this very wet year getting you down? If the answer to these and other situations is yes, can the situations be changed? If not, like the Salesian saint, why not accept it rather than waste the rest of the year or a career with complaints? Not only will it help you get through the day or the year, but this positive attitude will foster more student learning in your own classroom.

Our positive attitude can extend to our hopes and dreams for every individual student whom God has placed in front of us. My hope for each student to be the best she can be will only exist if I see the greatest potential of that student, the person that God meant for him to be. Bringing a joyful spirit to the classroom not only models joy for our students, but it also reduces tension for the task of learning. The French philosopher Voltaire, as cited in Gorrow (2004) said, "The most courageous decision one makes each day is the decision to be in a good mood" (p. 1).

Justice

"Teaching for joy and justice" is the name of an article written by Linda Christensen (2009). In it, she cites examples of ways teachers can incorporate practices that also promote justice. She believes that joy exists when teachers honor culture, race, native language, and family in student writing and projects, and when a student accomplishes something that he or she feels is beyond their capability. Christensen said she tries to "locate the curriculum in student's lives" (p. 52) because "I have discovered that students care more about learning when the content matters [to them]" (p. 50). When we put their world in the center of what we teach, we tell them their lives matter. This includes readings and texts that reflect a variety of diverse authors and experiences, and ones that reflect the challenges they face.

"Teaching for joy and justice also begins with the non-negotiable belief that all students are capable of brilliance" (Christensen, 2009, p. 50). Christensen, a high school teacher in a predominately African-American school in an urban, working class neighborhood, expresses her view that many times our students come from places of failure, both in their former classrooms and in their lives outside of school. Too often we blame them for arriving in our secondary classrooms without the tools they need to succeed academically. "My duty as a teacher," she said, "is to coax the brilliance out of them" (p. 50).

Laughter and Humor

One of the classes I taught in my first teaching job in a rural Ohio middle school was an all-boys foods class. For six weeks I taught them some of the basics of cooking and baking. One day the boys were working in small groups in their kitchens, making and baking brownies. All of a sudden, there was a burst of laughter from one of the kitchens. These boys were doubling over in laughter while one boy looked on in bewilderment, wondering what he was doing wrong. As I got closer to the source of the laughter, I saw that one young boy was holding a baking pan upside down and had literally buttered the outside bottom of the pan. He so innocently said, "The recipe said to butter the bottom of the pan." I soon realized he had followed the directions to a "t," maybe more than the way we normally butter the bottom of the pan! The young gentleman seemed to take the fun in stride, and when he realized why everyone was laughing, joined in himself.

I hope this former student didn't suffer from a roomful of laughter at his expense. Instead, I hope he is still telling this story as I am, many years later!

Enjoy yourself! There is joy in heaven, but there is also joy on earth. Ecclesiastes 3:4 states that there is a time for laughter. As Karl Barth said, "Laughter is the closest thing to the grace of God" (Quoteworld.org). And Brussat and Brussat said that "laughing is a spiritual practice." In the classroom we can smile more, laugh more, and use more humor. It can reduce tension, heal a hurt, open minds, and add joy to our lives. It can be a valuable teaching tool and should be used more regularly. Yet I don't remember ever receiving any inservice training or even encouragement to use this medium in the classroom.

Because I am so often task-oriented in class, I was surprised to receive an email from Jaime after a four-hour class with my cohort. She wrote, "I love being at Fox, and I am very grateful to have you as a cohort leader because I think you model a willingness to let us laugh and talk, but then you steer us in the right direction. So, thank you!" (JH email 9/16/09). My first reaction was that I must have not been task-oriented enough; my second reaction was that I needed to do this more often!

Many of our students don't experience joy in their lives outside of school. Rachael Kessler (2000) reminds us that many of them have been robbed of joy by difficult circumstances in their homes, or by pressures and dangers they live with on a daily basis. As a result, their natural instincts of a child's playfulness, spontaneity, silliness, and laughter are reduced or nonexistent. The classroom is a great place to share joy among and between its members. Foster an atmosphere of playfulness. Read a short poem that brings a smile, or tell a joke that relates (or not!) to the content. If we can laugh and have fun, our students will too. They will appreciate if we can add these components to the serious lessons they take part in each day. Kessler said that the hunger for joy and delight can be satisfied quite simply in the classroom through experiences such as "play, celebration, and gratitude" (p. 17). She suggested we share joyful events and life experiences, remind students that we are here to share our highs as well as our lows, invite humor, use rhythm and movement, foster moments of heartfelt connection with the group, and encourage the personal exhilaration when someone takes a new risk.

In your classroom, notice tiny epiphanies and little miracles: the patience of a third grader in drawing a flower, one student helping another with a math problem, a first grader lingering over an object another child brought to class, two seventh-grade girls kicking a soccer ball during lunch time, a student sharing part of her sandwich with another, or a high school group performing their "best ever" music program.

"A good laugh is sunshine in a house," William Thackeray once noted (www.brainyquote.com). Milton Berle, a comedian said "Laughter is an instant vacation." Wouldn't it be great if we could make sure each of our students laughed every single day! One elementary teacher I know has her students take a "boogie break" by putting on music and dancing for a few minutes. Students can let off steam, get some exercise, and hopefully experience some joy as well. A smile or chuckle may be just what someone needs. Laughter could take the edge off the work to do.

Teaching Effectiveness

I assume a classroom that fosters joy is also a classroom where learning occurs under the guidance of an effective teacher. Research increasingly ties student achievement to the quality of the teacher (Darling-Hammond, 2010; Goe & Stickler, 2008; Intrator, 2002). The evidence speaks to the importance of the teacher. Intrator (2002) said:

> If schools are to be places that promote academic, social, and personal development for students, everything hinges on the presence of intelligent, passionate, caring teachers working day after day in our nation's classrooms. Teachers have a colossal influence on what happens in our schools, because day after day, they are the ultimate decision makers and tone setters. They shape the world of the classroom by the activities they plan, the focus they attend to, and the relationships they nurture. (p. xxvii)

Effective teachers use a variety of teaching strategies to provide spaces where joy can be experienced. The following suggestions were made in articles that discussed ways to bring more joy into the classroom:

- Give choices to your students—being able to choose books, worksheets, and topics is a motivator.

- Play a game—it encourages playfulness, can build social skills, and reinforces academic content.

- Go outside more—it gives an opportunity to observe science and nature, as well as broaden a child's world.

- Do something kind for your students—write a quick note about something you've observed, a compliment, or something you appreciate.

- Read good books—it will open the world to someone who has had less privilege in life.

- Take a brain break or a boogie break—do exercises, move, or dance.

- Have students write cards and letters of appreciation to others and watch the joy it brings to those who write them as well as receive them.

- Transform assessments—use a variety of evaluations such as projects and posters.

- Offer more gym, art, and music classes.

- Make classroom environments more inviting—with color, student work, and student interests.

- Take time to tinker—provide common objects and time to create something with them

- Host festivities and invite others to join you.

- Toast moments of happiness you notice as you go through the day. (Hensley, 2008; Wolk, 2008)

Engaging the Soul

Both Palmer (2007) and Kessler (2000) talk about paying attention to the inner life and to nourishing the soul. The first time I read Kessler's book, *The Soul of Education*, was shortly after I left a public high school classroom. I had just taken a position at my Christian university. In her introduction, Kessler said that the title of her book might raise questions as to whether a public school education should even have a soul. Yes, we study mathematics, English, history and more. But doesn't the topic of soul belong in church and in private homes instead of in school? "If so," Kessler said, "someone had better tell the children" (p. ix). While we adults continue to debate this question, she reminds us that "most students continue to bring their souls to school" (p. ix).

The soul of a teacher has been influenced in another way. Palmer says, "We teach who we are" (2007, p. 1). By this, he means we are teachers made up of all the past and present experiences we have had in our lives, particularly those that have impacted our journey to become teachers. As a result, we entered the teaching profession with ideas of how we were going to function as a teacher. Along the way we faced external challenges, limitations, and inconsistencies that sometimes discouraged us because of inconsistencies with our original vision. We may have had to compromise or change directions from what we originally intended or hoped.

So where is joy in all of this? Joy rises up from within our souls, from our inner beings, from those places of disappointment and of pleasure (Intrator & Kunzman, 2006). If we ignore the soul in our own lives and in those of our students, we fail to make a connection between the person and the profession. We are also at risk of losing all inspiration in the face of our teaching realities. Even professional development should attend to the inner life of teachers, renewing ourselves, our purpose, and our commitment to God. Without renewal of our souls and spirits, we cannot experience or pass along this joy. And when we have it, John 16:22 tells us, "no one will take away your joy."

Parker Palmer wrote, "I am a teacher at heart, and there are moments in the classroom when I can hardly contain the joy" (2007, p. 1). Palmer speaks my desire. I want my life to be so full of God that my joy overflows from God through me to the students in my classroom. I pray that for me, as well as for you. May there be joy in our journeys!

Discussion Questions

Evaluate your attitude toward your students, and your colleagues. What, if anything, needs to change?

How do you promote justice in your classroom?

In what ways might you add humor, laughter, celebrations, and joy to your classroom?

Contemplate your soul, your inner life, and the teacher you are. Who are you? What do you want to be?

"Well done, good and faithful servant; you were faithful over a few things, I will make you ruler over many things. Enter into the joy of your Lord" (Matthew 25:21; NKJV). If we think we experience joy now, imagine the joy in heaven!

REFERENCES

Ball, A. (2001). *The saint's guide to joy that never fades.* Ann Arbor: Servant Publications.

Birky, V. (2001). *Perspectives of teacher leaders in an educational reform environment: Finding meaning in their involvement.* Unpublished doctoral dissertation, Oregon State University—Corvallis, OR.

Brussat, F., & Brussat, M. A. Laughing as a spiritual practice. In *Spirituality & Practice.* Retrieved from http://www.spiritualityandpractice.com/practices/features.php?id=20120.

Christensen, L. (2009). Teaching for joy and justice. *Rethinking Schools,* 23(4), 50–54.

Collins, M. G. (1998, March). Joy. *Forerunner, Bible Study.* Retrieved from http://www.bibletools.org/index.cfm/fuseaction/Library.sr/CT/BS/k/292/Joy.htm.

Daniels, H., and M. Bizar (2005). *Teaching the best practices way: Methods that matter, K-12.* Portland, ME: Stenhouse.

Darling-Hammond, L. (2000). Teacher quality and student achievement: A review of state policy and evidence. *Education Policy Analysis Archives,* 8(1).

———. (2010). *Evaluating teacher effectiveness: How teacher performance assessments can measure and improve teaching.* Retrieved from Center for American Progress website: http://www.americanprogress.org/issues/2010/10/teacher_effectiveness.html.

Ford, M. (1998, April). Joy and trial. *Forerunner, Ready Answer.* Retrieved from http://www.biblicaljesus.org/index.cfm/fuseaction/Library.sr/CT/RA/k/281/Joy-Trial.htm.

Goe, L., and L. M. Stickler (2008). Teacher quality and student achievement: Making the most of recent research. *National Comprehensive Center for Teacher Quality.* Retrieved from http://www.tqsource.org/publications/March2008Brief.pdf.

Gorrow, T. R. (2004). Rearrange your attitude: The art of being happy. *Classroom Leadership,* 8(1), 1–2.

Hazel, H. (2010). *The joy of teaching: Effective strategies for the classroom.* Eugene, OR: Pickwick Publications.

Hensley, P. (2009). 11 ways to bring joy into the classroom. *The Apple.* Retrieved from http://theapple.monster.com/benefits/articles/6303-11-ways-to-bring-joy-into-the-classroom.

Intrator, S. M. (2002). *Stories of the courage to teach: Honoring the teacher's heart.* San Francisco: Jossey-Bass.

Intrator, S., and R. Kunzman (2006). Starting with the soul. *Educational Leadership,* March 2006, 38–42.

Johnson, A. (2003). *The joy of teaching, or I want to run away and be a rock star.* [Keynote address] April 17, 2003, Weber State University Nye/Cortez Banquet.

Kessler, R. (2000). *The soul of education.* Alexandria, VA: ASCD.

Palmer, P. (2007). *The courage to teach: Exploring the inner landscape of a teacher's life*. San Francisco: Jossey-Bass.

Ritenbaugh, J. W. (1998, April). The fruit of the Spirit: Joy. *Forerunner, Personal*. Retrieved from http://www.cgg.org/index.cfm/fuseaction/Library.sr/CT/PERSONAL/k/280/Fruit-of-Spirit-Joy.htm.

S. M. (1011, January 21). *Trust and seek*. Newberg, OR: Your NFC.

Spiritual practices: Joy. *In Spirituality & Practice*. Retrieved from http://www.spiritualityandpractice.com/practices/practices.php?id=15

Teacher quality (2004, September 21). *Education Week*. Retrieved from http://www.edweek.org/ew/issues/teacher-quality/.

Thackaray, W. http://thinkexist.com/quotes/william_makepeace_thackeray/.

Wilson, M. B. (2010, April 2). The importance of joy. *Responsive Classroom*. (Blog post retrieved from http://www.responsiveclassroom.org/blog/importance-joy.

Wolk, S. (2008). Joy in school. *Educational Leadership*, 66(1), 8–15.

3

Discernment

MARC SHELTON

> If you've gotten anything at all out of following Christ, if his love has made any
> difference in your life, if being in a community of the Spirit means anything to you,
> if you have a heart, if you care—then do me a favor: Agree with each other, love each
> other, be deep-spirited friends. Don't push your way to the front; don't sweet-talk your
> way to the top. Put yourself aside, and help others get ahead. Don't be obsessed with
> getting your own advantage. Forget yourselves long enough to lend a helping hand.
> (Philippians 2:1–4, MSG)

HUMANKIND CONTINUES TO NEED such encouragement as the Apostle Paul gave to those living in Philippi around AD 61—living like Christ while acting like humans is sometimes paradoxical. Thus, this reminder is warranted in calling people to be mindful of the interests of others in our actions of living out our lives. Discernment in making decisions is an important biblical theme, given the fact that most of us act and interact as part of a larger community whether as a citizen, as an employee, or as a member of a family. The premise of this book is that Christians educators have something to say to encourage others in private and public settings that is informed by our life in Christ: to live life first as a follower of Christ and then as teachers, administrators, counselors, or school psychologists in our profession, which may also be our calling.

The theme of this chapter centers on leaders who enlarge conversations during decision making, understand situations more clearly from multiple perspectives, and thus make better decisions for organizations. But, this process is more than simply relying on our human abilities, knowledge, and personalities to discern what is best. Inviting God into the decision-making process both strengthens decisions and strengthens people, together in community. This biblical theme is found in 1 Corinthians 12:7–8: "Now to each one the manifestation of the Spirit is given for the common good. To one there is given through the Spirit a message of wisdom, to another a message of knowledge . . . , to another faith by the same Spirit . . ." We are stronger together by faithfully using Christ's gifts of wisdom and knowledge. Paul assures us that when we live like Christ, his Spirit brings gifts to our lives that bear fruit. These gifts help us to understand and employ many of the themes contained in this book, not just for the common good, but also for the glory of God (Galatians 5:22–23).

David encouraged his son with a similar focus on the common good when he charged Solomon to ask God for discernment to understand and know how best to lead Israel. Solomon, who would eventually be known as the wisest king of all, was encouraged to lead with a commitment to follow God. David spoke a word of blessing to Solomon that his leadership ". . . will have success if you are careful to observe the decrees and laws that the LORD gave Moses for Israel. Be strong and courageous. Do not be afraid or discouraged" (1 Chronicles 22:13). As this scripture illustrates, through faithfully listening to God's Spirit and with compassionate care for others, humans are capable of producing good and fruitful decisions in difficult situations when we strive to seek a clearer understanding.

School leaders have always worked to find strategies to communicate difficult decisions and to address perceptions of what constitutes transparent and open lines of dialogue—perceptions are reality, especially when it involves whether or not others believe they are properly informed or think they are correctly heard. It is from this context that I began considering the biblical theme of discernment and its application in the decision-making process employed by school leaders. As my thinking about discernment progressed through presentations and discussions with peers, who are preparing future leaders for service in schools, it became evident that discernment first begins in situations where we are challenged to understand how to provide adequate space for the conversation, and is then shaped by accurately determining when and anticipating which voices to invite.

Ideas from thinking about the how, when, and whom will come later in this chapter—for now it is important to clearly establish the focus as setting parameters for discernment in decision making and then to properly define discernment in the context of community where most educational decisions happen.

For the purpose of examining the biblical theme of discernment, I have chosen to focus on discernment in decision-making processes used by leaders in the school community. There are many pertinent examples that could be used in a chapter such as this, whether understanding how best to present a difficult lesson in the classroom or knowing the right words to diffuse a difficult situation with parents in the front office—in essence praying for God's guidance to give you a creative idea or just the right words. These are important tasks in our work as educators, but they tend to be limited to resolving a specific situation in a classroom or an issue with a specific family. It is important to remind readers to seek God's help in discerning how to best accomplish these tasks. But the focus of this chapter is on encouraging leaders to seek God's help to discern, to best understand and know how to resolve important, big-picture challenges. It is in this crucial work that discerning properly leads to making wise decisions for the common good—making knowledgeable decisions that represent all members of a school community.

DISCERNMENT IN DECISION MAKING DEFINED

Discernment is defined as the quality of being able to grasp and comprehend what is obscure; and the ability to see and understand people, things, or situations clearly and intelligently (Merriam-Webster Online)—through a keenness of intellectual perception (*Oxford Universal Dictionary*). Discernment assumes a certain knowledge or wisdom to apply perceptions appropriately when faced with dilemmas or difficult decisions. In situations that can significantly change an individual or an organization, discernment in decision making is more about taking time to keenly shape an informed judgment than to make hasty decrees.

This is where the important work of making decisions, which press the organization and its people to change, requires leaders to open up the process of discernment, especially in adaptive challenges as described by Ronald Heifetz (1994). But, leaders sometimes misinterpret interests of efficacy, efficiency, and expertise—repeating self-serving phrases such as 'I am the leader, so I must have the answers'—over encouraging decisions that are beneficial and fruitful to others. The "tyranny of the urgent" (Hummel, 1967) and self-promotion wins the day, instead of purposeful planning to make prudent decisions in a spirit of collaboration. It takes additional planning time and space to invite voices into the boardroom and into the principal's office, but it requires ample time and space to listen and discern well during the decision-making process, which can result in moving in a direction most meaningful and beneficial to the organization.

DECISION MAKING IN A BIBLICAL CONTEXT OF DISCERNMENT

It is important to define additional terms from a biblical perspective, as the term discernment can hold a spiritual connotation in the context of religious organizations (Fendall, Wood & Bishop, 2007). This allows room for believers to bring the spiritual into the perceived secular area of decision making, which is not predominant in the workplace. Although this context can be informed by the Christian view of the world, it is more a biblical implication for an educational process than an argument made from a theological perspective. This Christian worldview or belief informs our actions that pervade our work here at George Fox University: Christ is present in each of us, so Christ is present in our work. The term Christian, as used here, refers to one who believes in Jesus Christ; places one's faith, trust and obedience in Christ; is a Christ follower.

Our challenge as Christians is to stay involved in the decision-making process of our communities, whether the organization is Christian or not. For readers who are not in an organization that values faith, or specifically the Christian practice of discernment, the work of Parker Palmer (1998–1999) in the Seattle Public Schools is well documented, through the Teacher Formation Program. But, in my work of collaborating with private school leaders, honoring teacher voices and encouraging shared decision making is not always a strong standard just because the word "Christian" is on the side of the school's building or at the top of its letterhead.

Those who are followers of Christ have an additional responsibility in living a Christ-like life serving others and obeying God in that we are called to consider the interests of the others in decision making as encouraged by Paul in Philippians 2:4. Discernment in decision making, like one's calling, should arise from a strongly held personal belief where one is led by

Christ to see things clearly and to use our God-given talents and intellect to discern or perceive important mysteries. Being willing and able to take the next step of discernment by persuading colleagues to consider others' interests can lead to a breakthrough—this clarity of vision can help others see a solution within a difficult situation, and work with persistence to resolve a difficult challenge.

Discussion Questions

How do I bring the sacred into the secular in my work?

What spiritual disciplines are important to our community, and how do we reflect those in our practices?

INDIVIDUAL DISCERNMENT IN WORKPLACE DECISIONS

Individuals desire an opportunity to participate fully, or at least to the level of one's choosing, in the workplace, including organizational decision making. Work that is meaningful and rewarding creates satisfied workers (Sergiovanni, 1992), and processes that encourage shared decision making improve the opportunity to hear a broader range of voices speaking into decisions. Kutcher, Bragger, Rodriguez-Srednicki, and Masco (2010) researched the connection between faith and employee satisfaction and commitment to the workplace, invoking the term "organizational citizenship behavior" (p. 319). As Kutcher et al. suggest, these organizational behaviors are informed by employees' "religious beliefs (that) form their self-identities and guide their actions and decisions" (p. 335). Along this line, James Madison once stated, "In a free government the security for civil rights must be the same as that for religious rights" (Madison, 1788). This perspective also implies that proper self-government means pursuing opportunities for active and meaningful involvement in the workplace, and subsequently in its decisions. However, these actions should not be simply a matter of preference or come about by proclaiming a right; fruitful participation is really a moral obligation conducted out of one's sense of duty as an organizational citizen.

The English word 'citizen' is derived from the Latin word *civitas*, which is similar to 'civic.' If government is the structure or function of authority and controls to govern one's actions, then self-government is one's personal responsibility to control personal actions and private rights within corporate government, such as we accept by living as a citizen in a country and working in community with others within any organization. Citizenship is an important educational goal; citizens, who exercise individual rights especially by participating in decision making, enable society to benefit from their understanding and knowledge.

The Roman stoic-philosopher, statesman Cicero (106–43 BC), argued that rights and responsibilities of citizens were moral and natural, over legal and man-made, to be lived out in community within a social contract. This is an important distinction because personal action, regarding the virtues of wisdom (knowledge of both the divine and human) and prudence (the practical application of wisdom), is so important a theme to Cicero that he emphasized this concept of private care for the public good in a letter to his son referenced in his essay, *On Duty*:

> But that wisdom, which I have stated to be the chief, is the knowledge of things divine and human, which comprehends the fellowship of gods and men, and their society within themselves . . . it follows of course that the duty resulting from this fellowship is the highest of all duties. For the knowledge and contemplation of nature is in a manner lame and unfinished, if it is followed by no activity; now activity is most perspicuous when it is exerted in protecting the rights of mankind [care for the well-being of mankind]. (p. 113)

Living in community is what we are naturally created by God to do (Grenz, 1998), from the time of the first family. This purpose is reinforced by our country's unique declaration that "We hold these truths to be self-evident, that all men are created equal, that they are endowed by their Creator with certain unalienable Rights, that among these are Life, Liberty and the pursuit of Happiness" (U.S. Declaration of Independence, 1776). When leaders are aware of individual interests to meaningfully participate in decision making then employee satisfaction and well-being results. This phenomenon of including people in processes of discernment is popularly referred to as employee buy-in or more recently as vetting a decision, which improves the quality of organizational decisions, the quality of implementing those decisions by its employees, and eventually the quality of the place where individuals work.

The theory of site-based management and the practice of shared decision making is up for debate as to what degree it is present in an environment of high-stakes accountability and within the "buck-stops-here" mentality of boards of directors, but it does strengthen decisions by bringing them to the level where most decisions are implemented. Participatory decision making within a community not only values principles of a free society, it limits negative perceptions that decisions are being made "without our input," from the top down, which can have a detrimental effect on employee satisfaction, organizational culture, and workplace climate. Shared decision making also ensures that individuals flourish to be blessed and happy within an organization that values expertise, wisdom, and knowledge of others by inviting discernment into the process of making decisions—and encourages positive behavior from more of its citizens.

Discussion Questions

How willing am I to participate in decision making, and how willing am I to invest necessary time to listen well to others?

How do we respond when someone questions our decision-making process, or expresses concern that a decision was made without input?

UNDERSTANDING DISCERNMENT IN SCHOOL COMMUNITIES

An open and transparent decision-making process not only establishes controls to check power in educational organizations, it also creates opportunities for leaders to listen well to the needs of others. As most American schools exist to provide a service of educating children and adults, schools operate within a society that values, but does not mandate, individual participation in decision making, such as voting in a general election. Proper discernment includes an open process to create opportunities for students' voices to be heard in major classroom or school-wide policies and procedures, especially as they progress through to the post-secondary level.

Perhaps schools can respond to limit the criticism that 'my voice and opinions don't matter' by teaching and modeling the fact that self-government can and does make a difference through practicing the discipline of public involvement in community decisions. As most teachers and administrators are products of the American system of education, it follows that staff members in most schools expect an invitation to participate in decisions—to be part of the discernment in decision-making processes. Fruitful leaders discern what type of decisions to open up through an invitation to participate and which decisions are best made through a streamlined process.

As stated previously, an accepted goal of education is to ensure that children become productive and successful members of society—modeling that children have a voice in some classroom decisions may translate to increased participation in a society's organizations as adults. John Amos Comenius is noted for influencing the reform of human society through education, including the eventual system of American schooling. His was a world in the seventeenth century where religious and political strivings for allegiance and power led to war after war, instead of a society marked by a spirit of collaboration and discernment that shaped important decisions. This strife led to his philosophical foundation of pansophy (a universal wisdom or knowledge) in hopes of ending war or at least not perpetually fighting wars to resolve conflicts.

In his book, *The Great Didactic* (Didactica Magna), Comenius (1649) contended that ". . . the whole of the human race may become educated, men of all ages, all conditions, both sexes and all nations," which would mean that ". . . all men should be educated to full humanity—to rationality, morality, and happiness" (p. 11). He hoped this social reform led by education would lead to a unity of humanity by asserting:

> I call a school that fulfills its function perfectly, one which is a true forging-place: where the minds of those who learn are illuminated by the light of wisdom, so as to penetrate with ease all that is manifest and all that is secret, where the emotions and the desires are brought into harmony with virtue, and where the heart is filled with and permeated by divine love, so that all who are handed over to Christian schools to be imbued with true wisdom may be taught to live a heavenly life on earth; in a word, where all men are taught all things thoroughly. (p. 14)

Perhaps an education to "full humanity—to rationality, morality, and happiness" means an education that leads one to live as Christ in this world, but for what end? As an educational reformer John Comenius was far ahead of his time in viewing that a quality education could lead to a changed world.

He believed that teachers should understand how a child's mind develops and learns, which caused him to be convinced that all children should attend school and receive the same education about the civilization in which they live, so that they could understand and know how best to solve problems in society. In the same way, understanding and recognizing this important role and responsibility, which involvement in decision making offers people in a free society, should cause leaders to adopt a process that supports and encourages open discernment in decision making, to help people 'fulfill their function perfectly.'

A century after Comenius, this foundation of education was continued by James Madison (1788), who penned *The Federalist No.* 51, a paper titled *The Structure of the Government Must Furnish the Proper Checks and Balances Between the Different Departments*. Like Comenius, Madison saw the frailty of humans and stressed the importance of education through writings that proposed adding an element of checks and balances through government designed to ensure that the means of power and control lead to higher ends in society's decision making. More specifically, Madison stated, "But what is government itself, but the greatest of all reflections on human nature? If men were angels, no government would be necessary. If angels were to govern men, neither external nor internal controls on government would be necessary" (1788). Long before Madison realized the limits of human virtue, Paul wrote to remind his readers that, "Each of you should look not only to your interests, but also to the interests of others" (Philippians 2:4).

As we continue to think about discernment in the light of educational and political thinkers, we follow Comenius and Madison's line of reasoning that both these structures are important for life. We observe that governance structures in educational organizations are basic hierarchies—where boards control superintendents, superintendents control principals, principals control teachers, and teachers control students. These dual structures of education to fully develop human functioning and of government to control human shortcomings then require that people in each of these roles of authority see the need for establishing checks on making unilateral decisions, which serve to limit participation through self-serving interests for power.

People within organizations trust leaders to make decisions for them and for the good of others—to some just doing the work as assigned is satisfying enough. Others perceive that to live fully within an organization means being able to create, innovate, or to participate actively in decisions that will affect them personally. In this case, being included in a process to discern the best decision becomes more of a duty and a moral responsibility that can only be fulfilled by being able to participate in a discernment process. It is important learning to act on one's belief that opinions do matter, and more importantly believing that God may be speaking wisdom into the process of discerning the right course of action through individual members of the organization.

LEADERSHIP IMPLICATIONS FOR DISCERNMENT IN DECISION-MAKING

Understanding, recognizing, or anticipating that involvement in decision-making processes matters to some people are leadership skills best accomplished by an active and involved leader. If a leader accepts the premise that an individual's obligation to weigh-in on a decision should be recognized and protected, then there are leadership implications that are best informed through discerning the most appropriate style, skills, and decision-making process to implement as a leader by putting leadership theory into practice.

Leadership Style

Perhaps, servant leadership provides the best model for discernment in decision making. Robert Greenleaf (1977) implies that the complete range of human nature is reflected in the continuum between leader-first behavior, striving to achieve personal power or gain, and servant-first behaviors. This perspective requires leaders to strive for a more balanced approach or style:

> The difference manifests itself in the care taken by the servant-first to make sure that other people's highest priority needs are being served. The best test, and difficult to administer, is this: do those served grow as persons? Do they, *while being served*, become healthier, wiser, freer, more autonomous, more likely themselves to become servants? (p. 27)

Effective and successful leaders are those who best understand and know the needs of others and measure success through the lens of personal and professional growth of all people within the organization (Luthans, 2010). Leaders who encourage others to participate in decision making to resolve challenging situations ensure a broader understanding and knowledge that open the door to wisdom during this type of discernment process.

Larry Spears continued directing the work of The Greenleaf Center for Servant-Leadership after Greenleaf's death. Spears introduced the book he edited, *The Power of Servant Leadership* (Greenleaf, 1998), depicting how he sifted through the writings of Greenleaf to identify "ten characteristics of the servant leader" (p. 5), which shape leaders to lead from a servant-first perspective. The top two characteristics that Spears references for servant leadership are listening: "communication and decision-making skills . . . reinforced by a deep commitment to listening intently to others" and persuasion, defined as a

> reliance on persuasion, rather than on one's positional authority, in making decisions within an organization. The servant-leader seeks to convince others, rather than coerce compliance. This particular element offers one of the clearest distinctions between the traditional authoritarian model and that of servant-leadership. The servant-leader is effective at building consensus within groups. (p. 6)

Perhaps the major implication of using discernment in decision making is in the area of professional growth and development of leaders: both principal and teacher leaders. We tend to teach as we have been taught, so it follows that most of us lead in a style in which we have been led. Servant leadership is becoming more prevalent and utilizes a style of behaving as a leader that causes a leader to consider the interests of others, which in turn requires a leader to be willing to ask and then listen to others in the process for discernment in decision making.

Leadership Skills

Discerning when and how to create space and to plan time for shared decision making are important leadership skills, along with understanding who needs to be at the table. Fred Luthans (1988) researched the day-to-day work of managers to determine that effective principals operate mainly in two traditional management domains resulting in an organizational culture marked by high satisfaction, commitment, and performance: 1) completing tasks requiring content and craft knowledge; and 2) developing human resources through interpersonal relationships. However, these were not necessarily skills that resulted in the successful principal being promoted to positions "up and out"—up the organizational ladder based on understanding political landscapes and working the system leading to moving out of building-level leadership. But, effective and successful leaders also are able to understand the implications for involving others in decision-making processes by developing relationships within and outside of the school. A balanced leadership approach is one where leaders use skills to understand what needs to be done, know how best to accomplish organizational goals, and communicate this process to others: parents, teachers, and students (Luthans, 2010).

Discerning Which Type of Process

Although developing a style and utilizing skills conducive to positive behavior allow leaders to move from theory into fruitful practices, so does the ability to know and understand how to move from a traditional model of managing technical decisions. Challenges that will require an organization to adapt and change require an organization to use a more collaborative process of discernment in decision making. Ronald Heifetz (1994) addresses the difference between resolving technical challenges versus those situations that create adaptive challenges; it is through understanding and knowing these differences that leaders can provide a process leading to better discernment, which leads to making better decisions. These technical challenges can cause frustration and discomfort within an organization for a short period of time, but most people associated with the organization know that the expertise and resolve to find a solution already exists. An adaptive challenge is one that causes the organization to invest more time and attention to find a resolution because it is one that will result in significant change for individuals within the organization. Perhaps there is no decision that requires more discernment than a challenge that the school has not faced before or, worse yet, one where people are not yet aware of potential pitfalls and unintended consequences by making quick or wrong decisions.

Technical Challenges Require Technical Decisions

One mistake that leaders make is to convene a staff meeting to invite input on how to solve or discern technical challenges. It is in the process of making these decisions that leaders quickly find most people don't want to be involved or someone wants to be involved to a level that creates an entirely different challenge. For example, determining the bell schedule or class schedule is usually a technical challenge that is influenced by assessing available space in the facility, considering bus transportation systems including parent drop-off or pick-up procedures, working on the master-schedule logistics to resolve scheduling conflicts of teachers and rooms, or determining the time it takes students to move between classrooms with fewest disruptions. Convening a large meeting to hear from a variety of voices can only complicate this decision-making process. If the school leadership team knows what the issue is and technically how to best resolve it, then it becomes less difficult to determine who to invite to make the best decision to change the bell or class schedule. Most teachers trust administrators to convene the group that needs to be around the table, so decisions like this are often made in the summer before the school year starts. In the case of challenges requiring a technical solution, encouraging more people to get involved or lengthening the time to make sure opportunities for discernment happen will not result in making a better decision, but might lead to more frustration caused by people having to wait for something to happen.

In the area of technical decisions where the organization knows how best to resolve the situation, an open and transparent process is still beneficial to relieve the short-term frustration that people face, but the answer does not require much discernment as it is usually obvious once a small group collects data and analyzes the facts of the situation—a consensus decision-making model will only serve to add frustration within the organization. Most of these technical decisions come down to leaders just doing what leaders are supposed to do, so don't confuse the issue by acting in a way that suggests there may be larger implications that will change the organization through a long, drawn out process. The resolution is the key to stabilizing the temporary stress and it often provides a rewardable moment to recognize the good work of the person or team that resolved the challenge so quickly.

These are usually those decisions where people expect the leader to lead, and, as such, these challenges should be resolved sooner and more efficiently with less input needed to discern the best solution. By involving more people than is needed to resolve a technical challenge, the leader opens up the possibility that trust will be broken. Most evaluations of a leader's performance, both formally and informally, are based on the degree to which the leader does what has been promised or expected. Even though perception is reality in assessing this standard, personal integrity or lack thereof is either affirmed or laid out for all to see and judge. When people are asked for their input and they rightfully take time to participate in the process, the leader is often confronted with choosing competing options. So instead of picking one, the leader makes a different decision creating the appearance that the leader already determined the decision and wasted time asking for individual input. Since little discernment is needed to resolve a technical challenge, I have observed where this error can cause fewer people to get involved in future decision-making processes. This is especially detrimental when important decisions arise that could change the structure of an organization.

Adaptive Challenges Require Discerned Decisions

It is in these decisions, where people within the organization will be required to adapt, that leaders make consequential mistakes. Leaders unaware of when to convene a process to encourage discernment, try to apply the same process as used in technical challenges. The leader has potentially lost trust before the decision-making process lifts off the ground, as a select group is convened to make a hasty decision to get on with more important stuff. Those decisions to address challenges that will significantly change an organization are best made through a strategically planned process, allowing for additional time and space to hear multiple perspectives.

For the purpose of discussing a scenario that creates an adaptive challenge for a school, let's assume that we are rethinking the bell or class schedule because we are considering a move to proficiency-based education at a secondary school or in blended grade levels at an elementary school. This consideration changes the challenge from a technical decision to one that will create a change in the school's basic structure: the classroom. Immediately, there will be questions of why this change is being considered and who will make the final decision, which is a good indication that this will require people within the community to adapt to a significant change; it is more than just deciding how to adjust the bells, so it requires a discernment process to include perspectives representative of all groups within the organization. It will also require leaders to anticipate who to include in the decision-making process, or others who may be impacted by this decision within and outside of the school community.

Without addressing the details that would take leaders within a school system at least a couple of months to plan in process alone, I provide a couple of considerations to demonstrate the magnitude of such an adaptive challenge. This also serves to reinforce why discernment needs to infuse the entire process within the context of shared decision making, a process that should be expanded far beyond what is required for making technical decisions. The initial level of planning relates to considering the immediate question posed by the community: Why? Prior to announcing the plan for the decision-making process, the teaching and support staff, parents, students, and the superintendent and governing board (if this change hasn't been directed by them), will want to hear the issue presented with facts and rationale for why the change is needed. This step is already evident in a technical challenge as those appear front and center begging to be resolved; a technical challenge is similar to getting a flat tire on your car as we don't have to know why it happened, but we need to know how to fix it to get back on the road as soon as possible.

An adaptive change is not so obvious, so even before answering the question of why, leaders should have floated the idea to prepare people within the community for change. Professional learning communities within schools provide staff time and resources to consider options. Common readings on the educational benefits to student learning and barriers to implementation provide an opportunity to look at the issue using a 360-degree approach (Hord, 1997). A town-hall concept with parent groups and meetings in the larger community can be beneficial to the process of presenting facts and the rationale, as well as providing a forum to listen to the perspectives of others. Perhaps the largest consideration requiring discernment in this decision will be the professional training required to implement such a change in instruction and content delivery; teachers will need to understand how proficiency-based learning at the middle school or in blended grade levels in our elementary classrooms will change teaching and learning. Most of all, this will take time and money, both precious resources for schools today. So, making sure that people have been part of a process to discern the best way forward is critical to prepare to best implement the decision.

Decisions leading to change is no less a time to lead. It is not a time to abdicate leadership responsibilities, as formal leaders are important to the success of implementing decisions (Elmore, 1979–80). Remember, adaptive challenges require multiple perspectives, and are best heard in a decision-making process that includes time and space for discernment by people who want to participate in these decisions. These types of decisions require leaders to use a differentiated leadership style to discern which employees to invite into the discussion, and when and how to initiate the process based on the situation (Hersey & Blanchard, 2000). There is a tool to help leaders determine which staff members express interest in being involved in various roles of leadership, including participating in open decision-making processes (Birky, Shelton, & Headley, 2006, p. 98). Expanding leadership opportunities to others who wish to participate in a process to discern the best way forward, a process typically limited to administrators, not only provides opportunities for multiple voices to be heard in the process of discernment, but reduces stress on administrators by lightening the load and isolation inherent with personally owning a unilateral decision.

This discernment process changes the context—from limiting understanding and restricting involvement in a decision by restricting the process to fewer eyes, ears, and brains to sharing the making of decisions to discern the best steps to resolve a situation. The willingness of leaders to change the process to include discernment in decision making results in stronger decisions that represent shared values more aligned to the organization's purpose as demonstrated by its mission and goals, both in its operations and in its decision-making process.

Discussion Questions

What is my preferred leadership style and what would people say is my actual leadership style—leader first or servant first, participatory or take-charge?

How do we decide whom to involve in our decision-making process?

Share a time when you participated in a collaborative decision, and describe the process and outcome.

CONCLUDING THOUGHTS ON DISCERNMENT IN DECISION-MAKING

Hopefully, presenting a perspective suggesting discernment in decision making is an encouragement—a call to consider the interests of others and to seek God's guidance to make wise decisions. Leading from a style of acting as a servant first; responding effectively to adaptive challenges by properly understanding how these decisions will change and shape people within organizations; and incorporating spiritual disciplines in leadership experiences of everyday life is not necessarily a default perspective. Lest we make the mistake that faithful teaching invokes a narrow view that focuses on one faith tradition, many faith backgrounds facilitate discernment in decision making and teach that beliefs should inform daily practices.

In current discourse, there are those who would say that spiritual disciplines, such as discernment, have no place in the forum of public or even private conversations, including decision making. Seeing one's actions as moral obligations—as a contributing member of society within organizations—is not a topic included in many leadership texts (Sergiovanni, 1996) and a viewpoint that can anger those who interpret any expression of faith as suspect in the public arena. A recent opinion piece in *The Wall Street Journal* quoted a United States representative, who cited teaching that has informed actions of individuals within civic organizations, churches, and charities dating back to 1891:

> A person's faith is central to how they conduct themselves in public and in private. So to me, using my Catholic faith, we call it the social magisterium, which is how do you apply the doctrine of your teaching into your everyday life as a layperson . . . where we interact with people as a community, that's how we advance the common good. (p. A15)

The unity that comes by living faithfully in alignment with Christ and others is not just theoretical but is foundationally practical; it should not be reserved for only religious roles, but in secular roles as it affirms that Christ is present in each of us, so Christ is present in our common work of caring for the common good through discernment in community decisions. It is the hope that we have in the message of the Gospel that teaches us to have faith in God and to act on that faith in working with others—to be lovers of God and lovers of people, as he promises to guide us with our decisions in life (Proverbs 3:6).

Art Kleiner (2008) uses religious nomenclature in his book, *The Age of Heretics*, to describe the work to move organizational behavior away from scientific measurements to social interactions where relationships matter. Moving to this relational process may cause one to pay more attention to the voice of the few who are discerning differently the best direction. And it may cause an organization to focus less on effectiveness, efficiency, and productivity and more on work that is meaningful, beneficial, and fruitful to measure success—measures that have faith-based roots, as presented in the letter to the church at Philippi (Philippians 4:8) and others throughout the New Testament. Kurt Lewin (1939), whose social psychology theories shaped current perspectives on organizational culture, coined the term "democratic leadership" to describe skills leaders' use through participatory decision making to positively encourage engagement and maintain motivation (Bavelas & Lewin, 1942). Again, as Thomas Sergiovanni (2006) postulates, "What is rewarding gets done" (p. 26), perhaps even with a better quality in the end than work that is rewarded.

In educating our children and in working together with other adults in the collaborative and relational work of education, ours is a twofold purpose. First, we strive to work well to prepare future generations with the knowledge, skills, and abilities to be self-governed in a civilized society. But it is also an important endeavor to model listening to Christ to be led to work well with each other in making decisions based on a collective process of discerning together in community that seeks the "mind of Christ" (1 Corinthians 2:16). Living as followers of Christ helps lead to unity and love, as later in 1 Corinthians, Paul describes the interworking of our body to compare this to our life in community, whether in churches or in schools. What is our motivation in expanding the voices in the room during those decisions that will lead to significant change in an organization? It may be that through listening well to God, it causes us to listen well to each other; listening with discernment to hear and see God in others persuades us to work together to make the best and most honorable decisions. Perhaps this will help humans flourish in this life to get the most out of a life of following Christ, leading to blessing and happiness.

REFERENCES

Bavelas, A., and K. Lewin (1942). "Training in Democratic Leadership." *The Journal of Abnormal and Social Psychology*, 37(1), 115–19.

Birky, V. D., M. Shelton, and W. S. Headley (2006). "An Administrator's Challenge: Encouraging Teachers to Be Leaders. *NASSP Bulletin* 90(2), 87–101.

Cicero, M. T. (1902) *De officiis (On duty).* In Arthur L. Humphreys ed., *Cicero: De Officiis.* London: Editor.

Comenius, J. A. (1649). *The Great Didactic (Didactica Magna).* London: Roehampton University. Retrieved from http://core.roehampton.ac.uk/digital/froarc/comgre/.

Elmore, R. F. (Winter, 1979–1980). "Backward Mapping: Implementation Research and Policy Decisions. *Political Science Quarterly*, 94, 601–16.

Fendall, L., J. Wood, and B. Bishop (2007). *Practicing Discernment Together: Finding God's Way forward in Decision Making.* Newberg, OR: Barclay.

Greenleaf, R. K. (1977). *Servant Leadership: A Journey into the Nature of Legitimate Power and Greatness.* Mahwah, NJ: Paulist.

Greenleaf, R. K. (1998). *The Power of Servant Leadership.* San Francisco, CA: Berrett-Koehler.

Grenz, S. J. (1998). *Created for Community: Connecting Christian Belief with Christian Living.* Grand Rapids: Baker Academic.

Heifetz, Ronald A. (1994). *Leadership without Easy Answers.* Cambridge, MA: Belknap.

Henninger, D. (2012, April 12). "Demolishing Paul Ryan." *The Wall Street Journal*, p. A15.

Hersey, P., and K. H. Blanchard (2000). *Management of Organizational Behavior: Utilizing Human Resources* (8th ed.). Englewood Cliffs, NJ: Prentice Hall.

Hord, S. M. (1997). *Professional Learning Communities: Communities of Continuous Inquiry and Improvement.* Austin: Southwest Educational Development Laboratory.

Hummel, C. E. (1967). *Tyranny of the Urgent.* Downers Grove, IL: InterVarsity.

Kleiner, A. (2008). *The Age of Heretics: A History of Radical Thinkers Who Reinvented Corporate Management* (2nd ed.). San Francisco, CA: Jossey-Bass.

Kutcher, E. J., J. D. Bragger, O. Rodriguez-Srednicki, and J. L. Masco (2010). "The Role of Religiosity in Stress, Job Attitudes, and Organizational Citizenship Behavior. *Journal of Business Ethics*, 95, 319–37.

Lewin, K., R. Lippitt, and R. K. White (1939). "Patterns of Aggressive Behavior in Experimentally Created "Social Climates." *Journal of Social Psychology*, 10, 271–301.

Luthans, F. (1988). "Successful vs. Effective Real Managers." *Academy of Management Executive,* 2(2), 127–32.

Luthans, F. (2010). *Organizational Behavior* (12th ed.). New York: McGraw-Hill.

Madison, J. (1788) *The Federalist No. 51: The Structure of the Government Must Furnish the Proper Checks and Balances between the Different Departments.* Retrieved from http://www.ourdocuments.gov/doc.php?flash=true&doc=10&page=transcript.

Palmer, P. J. (Dec. 1998/Jan. 1999). "Evoking the Spirit in Public Education." *Educational Leadership*, 56(4), 6–11.

Sergiovanni, Thomas (1996). *Moral Leadership: Getting to the Heart of School Improvement.* San Francisco, CA: Jossey-Bass.

4

Hospitality

Shary Wortman

Located in a neighborhood with many rentals and motels, a school with a mobility rate of over 30 percent yearly welcomed many new students into the classrooms each week. For some of these students, the school was the fifth or sixth school they had attended. The staff saw the need to construct a plan that would help the new students easily transition into the school. They created a "Welcome Packet" that contained coupons new students could redeem for gifts from school personnel. The principal presented a pencil, the librarian furnished a bookmark, the custodian provided an eraser, and the cafeteria worker offered a cookie. When introduced to the counselor, a new student was interviewed about interests and favorite things, and then the counselor took a picture of the student and posted it on the front entrance bulletin board so the community could learn more about the new student and extend a welcome. Student "greeters" from each classroom met the new student, took him on a tour of the building to meet the many adults and to redeem the coupons. The greeters accompanied the new student to lunch and recess and acted as a tour guide showing and sharing things that would lead to success in the new school. The staff discovered that students made friends much faster and became more confident in their classrooms quicker than before they implemented this plan. Teachers told endless stories about the lack of fear they saw in new students because of these greeters.

I remember a new student's parent, with tears in her eyes, coming to me the day after she enrolled her child. She shared that because of her husband's work, they had to move often and so her child had been in over ten schools. She went on to say that her son had never wanted to come back to the new school the second day and usually came home crying. In our school, the parent said, he met important school personnel, received gifts and was enjoying two new friends. This parent talked at length expressing the guilt she and her husband felt over the negative impact of their frequent moves upon the family. It was affirming to hear her words and to know that making some changes in how we welcome our students to our school, and intentionally extending hospitality, made a difference in our students' lives.

This chapter reflects the many facets of hospitality and the different ways we view and practice it in our daily lives as educators. Perhaps you will find a new purpose in your teaching as you explore how hospitality can play a part in your classroom and contribute to your effectiveness as a teacher. We may never know the far-reaching impact of our hospitable actions towards others, but as we consider the message of Jesus, we can examine how we might "walk the talk" of Christian hospitality. Within this chapter, we will reflect on how hospitality can create a welcoming and caring learning environment that profoundly affects the successes of students in our classrooms.

How shall we define hospitality? Webster (1996) defines hospitality as "the act, practice or quality of being friendly and showing care, concern towards another's health and happiness" (p. 297). According to Anderson (2011) during the early centuries of Christian era, the Greek root in words translated as "hospitality" or "hospitable" in the New Testament is *philoxen*, literally meaning "fond of strangers or guests" (p. 16).

Anderson (2011) states, "The hospitality envisioned, especially as applied to the classroom setting, is an intentional practice that reflects a process and perspective rather than specific tasks teachers must add to their already overtaxed schedules" (p. 13). With the rigor of testing, benchmarks, and adequate yearly progress, teacher accountability is in the spotlight. Hospitality is not an "add on" to the teachers job; it is the "mode of operation" or the essence of how the teacher teaches. It is how the teacher honors people and develops relationships. It is how the teacher takes advantage of the opportunities to relate to students and build connections. It is the demonstration of an attitude of unconditional acceptance and love that comes from the heart of the teacher.

In discussing hospitality and its biblical applications with our oldest daughter, Tiffany, she made an important connection for me. She said, "Jesus went on the 'ultimate road trip' during his life on earth, extending hospitality to all." She continued to say, "In our roles as educators and teachers, hospitality is part of the foundation of our work which reflects our attitude and how we do our work to help and support students and colleagues on their journey or road trip to reach their optimum potential." How we manifest hospitality in our classroom is at the heart of teaching. For each of us, the defining terms and meaning may vary. The definition of hospitality, through the context of Christianity and Jesus' teachings, reveals the importance of making hospitality part of how we go about our business in our classroom and how "we walk our talk."

Biblical stories offer ways to make connections to Christian hospitality in our work as teachers and makes increasingly clear that extending this hospitality is an educational responsibility. Jesus used hospitality to honor and develop relationships with others. He also took risks and embraced opportunities to comfort and connect with others and to ultimately teach the importance of unconditional love. Teachers are charged with the mandate to build relationships within our classrooms and schools.

Discussion Questions

As you think of hospitality, what does it mean to you?

What makes you feel cared for and welcomed by someone?

How has your definition of hospitality changed
over your years of teaching?

What does the connection between relationship
and hospitality mean to you?

HOSPITALITY AS RELATIONSHIPS AND INCLUSION

Nurturing and developing relationships represents the heart of hospitality. Building connections fosters community and acceptance. In the classroom, when we take time to tell stories and share life lessons, we develop connections with our students and others. Through stories, we learn about our students' lives beyond the classroom. The students also learn about and identify with others and discover things they have in common.

I remember by name those teachers who made an exceptional connection with me. One such teacher, Mrs. Wells, would make a special bagged lunch each week for a different student in our first-grade class. We all waited with anticipation, and when it was our turn, we would move our chair next to her big desk and open the brown paper bag containing the lunch she had made with care. There was always something unique in the lunch. When it was my turn, Mrs. Wells brought some fresh carrots from her garden and an apple from her fruit trees. During this lunch, Mrs. Wells asked if I would like to be one of dancers who would dance around the May Pole at our annual May Day Celebration. That was like being asked if I wanted to be a queen. She also asked about my pet dog and our other farm animals. During the school day, we hardly ever had the chance to talk to her about our personal lives, let alone have her ask questions about our pets and the things we loved. Mrs. Wells was able to form a bond between her students and herself, and it encouraged our best work. I still remember her today, fifty-nine years later, and her caring and welcoming attitude and the relationship I had with her. She was a teacher who made all students feel special, cared for, and supported. The little things she did made a difference. She found out about our personal interests, our home life, and had conversations with us about the important parts of our lives. She was a wise teacher who practiced hospitality in many ways.

In the classroom where every student comes with unique gifts and talents, the teacher must recognize that although each student's contribution may be somewhat different from those of the other students, all contributions should be recognized, appreciated, and celebrated daily. This is our challenge as Christian educators—to have a heartfelt attitude of inclusiveness for all students by creating an environment of Christian hospitality that will convey welcome, acceptance and belonging to all we encounter. Sometimes students who are difficult "guests" in our classrooms challenge us when it comes to the practice of hospitality. Christian teachers must remember Peter's advice to practice hospitality ungrudgingly, without grumbling, and out of love and openhearted sincerity (1 Peter 4:9). We must never give up on our students, but we must also recognize that we represent only one place on their life journey, and yet we can be the teacher who makes a difference.

I know that outside of our schools there exists the real world where fear, biases, and prejudice still live, waiting to be healed by education and Christian teachings. As teachers, we must clearly convey to our students that unkind words, name-calling, teasing, harassing, or any form of ridicule have no place in our world and certainly not the classroom. Through building understanding and respect for others, the teacher can act as an example to helping promote cultural competence and understanding. With this knowledge one can build acceptance and respect for others.

In Mark, Jesus said, "For even the Son of Man did not come to be served, but to serve . . ." (Mark 10:45). Jesus describes everyday acts of hospitality toward people who were strangers, diseased, poor, hungry, imprisoned, and disabled. Jesus reminds us that when we practice hospitality, we should do it as if we were doing it for him. In Matthew, Jesus said that in welcoming the least of these, we actually welcome Him (Matthew 25:44–45). When we apply these passages to our lives as educators, we transfer the idea of justice into the classroom. Jesus was concerned for the poor, strangers, widows, orphans, the disabled, and the sick. Teachers, by their own actions, promote justice in their classrooms and act as a conduit for making connections between students of varying ability levels or children who differ in socioeconomic status, ethnic, and racial backgrounds. Everyone has gifts and struggles. Some manifest to the physical "outer" presence of a person, but Christian teachers recognize this and strive to provide inclusive classrooms where they affirm the dignity and equality among all students regardless of the type of ability.

There are many examples in the Bible of how Jesus treated others who were different from him. In John, we read about a woman who was a Samaritan—a member of the ostracized mixed race who had a bad reputation—and who was in a public place. No respectable Jewish man would talk to a woman under such circumstances (John 4:1–42). But Jesus did. We must extend hospitality to all, no matter what his or her race, social position, or past sins. Jesus crossed all barriers. We who follow him must act as extensions of His love and hospitality. Of course, the ultimate guideline for hospitality is found in Matthew: "So in everything, do to others what you would have them do to you, for this sums up the Law and the Prophets" (Mathew 7:12). It also serves us well as we look at how we honor people and build relationships in our classrooms.

Sometimes students have challenges that seem overwhelming and we feel unable to effectively work with these students in a way that demonstrates hospitality. Only much later do we realize that God sent these students to us as a blessing in disguise to teach us lessons about life and how to grow and how to serve others. In some situations, God has to stretch us in order to bring the lesson home. God may intentionally bring us to our knees with challenges before he lifts us to our feet with opportunities that help us understand that as teachers, we are life-long learners, and he is the guide by our side. In our roles as educators and teachers, we dedicate our work to helping and supporting our students and others on their educational journey to becoming the most effective person possible, regardless of the challenges with which they enter our care. We hold the privilege of building relationships and instilling feelings of acceptance within our students. Many times, we do not get to follow through with our students after they move on from our program or classrooms. Our heartfelt wish is that we have created a space where relationships are nurtured and students feel accepted, included, and cared for in our classrooms.

Discussion Questions

How has hospitality helped build brotherhood and a relationship between you and someone who may be very different than yourself?

Can you think about a time in your teaching or job when you have been challenged to love someone who seems unlovable? How did you work through this situation?

How do you reflect Christian hospitality in your classroom practices and expectations?

What are some ways you can honor all students?

What does Jesus tell us about diversity?

How might you show hospitality to an adversarial parent or student?

HOSPITALITY AS ENCOURAGEMENT AND SUPPORT

Opportunities can often involve some risk. When my husband coached our daughter's softball teams, he encouraged the girls by stating, "You can't steal second base if you keep your foot on first." Now, as I have watched my three grandsons play sports, I admire their energy and their drive to take risks as they learn new ways to play the games. They gladly participate at a field or gymnasium full of onlookers and try out new skills. They enjoy the encouragement of their teachers and coaches. They make mistakes and become embarrassed, but they come back time and time again regardless of the challenge and the unsuccessful attempts because they feel welcomed to do so. As teachers, we need to encourage our students to take advantage of opportunities and not fear taking some risks. By giving praise and encouragement to not give up whenever opportunities hold challenges, students may come to view trials as natural learning experiences and grow in their wisdom.

I have seen teachers continue to encourage their students to take risks and try new things even when students are presented opportunities for which they are fearful. I recall a beloved PE teacher who designed a ropes course for our middle school students. When the course was completed, I looked at the maze of ropes strung from tree to tree 20 feet above the ground and it made me quiver as I watched students challenge themselves to complete the course. Over the next several weeks, confidence blossomed, peers cheered each other with words of encouragement, and students where heard saying, "I didn't think I could do it, but I did." This teacher built trusting relationships among his students, provided the opportunities for them to take some risks, honored all students' accomplishments, and welcomed all to try. His outdoor classroom truly was an inclusive classroom where all students felt safe, cared for, and respected.

The author of Hebrews directed his readers not to be afraid to show hospitality to strangers by reminding them that "by so doing some people have entertained angels without knowing it" (Hebrews 13:2). One Christmas, a fifth-grade teacher planned a service project with her class and asked children to collect clothing items for a homeless man who often sat outside a neighborhood grocery store collecting pop cans that he could redeem for the deposit. The teacher drove to the grocery store to deliver the gifts and she asked the man how he was doing. He said with a smile, "Too blessed to complain." She told him about her students and then invited him to the classroom for their Christmas party. Then without thinking, she put her arms around him and hugged him tightly. His body fell limp in her arms and his eyes filled with tears. She was overwhelmed with the wonder of when he might have last had someone hug him.

We underestimate the power we have as human beings and teachers. The encouraging words, the touch on the shoulder, the listening ear, the heartfelt compliment, and a smile of confidence are all ways to extend hospitality and move people in unexpected ways. These acts of acceptance and hospitality have the potential to make a difference in a person's life and in our lives. I strongly feel we make a living by what we get and make a life by what we give. A homeless man was a teacher and made someone think of what true hospitality can mean to another human being. Sometimes we are very cautious about when and how we extend hospitality—fearful in reaching out to strangers.

Discussion Questions

Can you think of times when God has presented an opportunity for you to extend hospitality, but you did not act?

Have you taken some risks in showing hospitality? How did it turn out?

Have you ever been entertained by an angel who showed you hospitality?

How do you provide a welcoming environment for students to take risks?

Is your teaching style hospitable to different kinds of learners?

HOSPITALITY AS SERVICE AND SACRIFICE

In the Gospel of John, chapter 12, we read the story of the art of hospitality and how Jesus taught others lessons about hospitality. Making sure a guest feels welcomed, warmed and well fed requires creativity, organization and teamwork. Mary and Martha's ability to accomplish this makes them the best sister hospitality team in the Bible. Jesus often stayed in their home. For Mary, hospitality meant giving more attention to the guest than worrying about making the proper preparations for company. Mary was more interested in her guest's words than in the cleanliness of her home or timeliness of her meals. She let her sister Martha take care of those details.

Mary acted as a mainly "responder." Mary had a deep concern for people's feelings. She focused on preparation more than participation.

Unlike her sister, Martha worried about details. She wished to please, to serve, to do the right thing, but she often succeeded in making everyone around her feel uncomfortable. Martha expected others to agree with her priorities and was overly concerned with doing everything right. She tended to feel sorry for herself when her efforts were not recognized. Perhaps she was the oldest and felt especially responsible, so she tried too hard to have everything perfect. Mary's lack of cooperation bothered Martha so much that she finally asked Jesus to tell Mary to help. Jesus gently pointed out that Mary was actually doing her part.

Each sister had her own lesson to learn. Mary learned that worship sometimes involves service. Martha learned that obedient service often goes unnoticed. The last time she appears in the Gospels, she is again serving a meal to Jesus and the disciples—this time without complaint. Martha and Mary were hospitable homeowners and friends of Jesus. They believed in him with growing faith. An important lesson to learn from this story is that getting caught up in details can make us forget the main reasons for our actions. When Jesus visited Mary and Martha, he did not chastise Martha for working, but for worrying. He told her that she was anxious and troubled about many things but at that moment she just needed to enjoy his visit. Martha needed to give herself permission to "lighten up". All the things she worried about were not the things worth worrying about. The perfect house was not that important, and what Mary was doing was not something with which Martha should be concerned herself. She needed to relax and enjoy the miracle of the moment. Jesus had come to her house. Even though she needed to make some preparations, she did not need to lose her peace. There is a proper time to listen to Jesus and a proper time to work for Him.

In our classrooms, we sometimes strive for perfection and spend hours worrying about things not worth the worry. As a principal, I worked with a teacher who was a perfectionist and spent hours before and after school and on weekends preparing for her students. She spent more time at school than at her home. Her home life became a disaster and her relationships with her family suffered. The teacher she team-taught with had learned early in his teaching career that he needed balance in his life and he identified the priorities in his teaching and in his home life, and worked at keeping the proper perspective as he planned, worked, and played. During the school year as we all worked together, it became an apparent for the perfectionist that she was getting caught up in too much detail and that made her forget the main reasons for her actions. With help from others, she made progress in setting priorities and maintaining balance in her life. She learned she could not give her best to students if she was not at her best. We must not forget to give hospitality to ourselves, so that may give it to others.

As teachers, we need to remember the importance of balance when we work with busy schedules and rigorous class expectations. When we feel exhausted and lack strength, endurance, vigor and energy, we run out of patience and tolerance and cannot think as clearly or perform as strongly as needed by our students. Extending hospitality becomes very difficult for exhausted teachers. God reminds us to balance serious-minded, sober, disciplined, prudent and diligent work with rest. We need refreshment not only physically, but also mentally and emotionally. In today's world, with the busyness and feelings of exhaustion, we sometimes lose the balance between work and rest. We long for time with friends and family and time for moments to ourselves. We long for a time when we could extend hospitality. If our bodies are overburdened, weary and tired, we need to create time for rest, delight and renewal—a refuge for our souls. Jesus speaks of how we can use this time of sacred rest to refresh our bodies and minds, restore our creativity and regain our inner self so we might be better able to serve others (Matthew 11:28–30).

Discussion Questions

What were the barriers that can stop us from acting hospitable?

Can you think of a time when you were not willing or able to accept hospitality from another person? Why do you think that it was difficult for you to accept hospitality?

In extending acts of hospitality, have you ever found yourself similar to Martha or to Mary?

When you are preparing to offer hospitality in your classroom, what are the things you to do prepare?

In the many roles you share along with being a teacher, what are the things you are doing to give you balance and rest in your life?

HOSPITALITY AS KINDNESS

Nouwen (1975) describes hospitality as a "fundamental attitude toward others that finds its expression in various ways. How a teacher articulates it in the classroom will be colored by the personality and teaching style of the teacher" (p. 67). Our capacity to do good work comes from recognizing who we are and our transparency with students and others about those beliefs. Many biblical stories of hospitality focus on entertaining strangers and vulnerable or ostracized people. Similarly, we have marginalized students in our classrooms who feel hostility rather than hospitality at school due to bias and uninformed or fearful attitudes that result in unjust treatment by others students and teachers. Rather than a series of tasks to be performed, or simply receiving strangers into one's home or classroom, hospitality is a way of life to be embraced by following Jesus. Hospitality begins with who you are at the core and reflects how you view yourself, your life, your world and others. It requires a disposition of justice and kindness.

David W. Anderson (2011) focuses on the idea that "attempts to promote inclusion of students with disabilities have often resulted merely in physical access to general education classrooms. But, this does not guarantee that these students are welcomed and treated kindly as an equal part of the classroom community" (p.14). When we see what happens in inclusive classrooms, we see the teacher focusing on the strengths and needs of all students in the classroom. The teacher in an inclusive classroom makes sure everyone's unique gifts and talents are recognized, accepted and celebrated. Just because some of our students have access to a special education classroom does not automatically mean the classroom is inclusive and radiates with hospitality or kindness. We need to remember that accessibility and hospitality are not the same. Hospitality can be seen in the teacher's approach to students and how the classroom environment conveys welcome, acceptance, and belonging to all students.

In one of my first schools where I served as principal, family incomes were among the lowest in the district with many of our single parents unemployed. Several of our students lived with their grandparents. Because of our lower enrollment, our school housed the district's special education classes. Students meeting special education qualifications were transported to our school from all the other schools in order to have access to the resources housed in our location. At this time, special education was considered a pullout program from the general education classrooms. Hosting the special education program in our school enriched the rest of the school population because of we were able to teach important life skills about working with others, including the importance of kindness in our interactions.

Some of the students had been diagnosed with Down's syndrome, others were students with autism, and another child was in a wheelchair and tube-fed. The list could go on. Teachers intentionally planned activities that allowed all students to help each other learn. The activities involved simple skills such as measuring, reading the weather gauge, or setting the table to more advanced skills involving reading, playing a flute, or learning how to play tetherball and hopscotch. An important benefit was the acceptance all students learned from understanding each other's uniqueness. With time, children didn't seem to notice the drooling or tilted head of the child in the wheelchair, the difficulty some had with speech, the disfigured bodies, and the many other differences that were outwardly apparent in physical appearance. Students began to look inside the other because teachers had provided the environment that nurtured the many aspects of hospitality.

Modeling hospitality and kindness can also involve the larger community. I co-taught with another teacher during some of my years of teaching at the elementary level. We realized that many of our students did not have grandparents who were part of their lives, so we decided to find some "seniors" who would come into our classroom and possibly teach a special skill they had and then eat lunch with us. The seniors came with many years of experience, stories and talents. We initially thought this would answer a need for some of the students in the form of an additional adult to listen, care for them, and validate their gifts. But as time went on, we discovered it also provided a place for our seniors to feel valued and needed as they shared their talents. We created the environment of hospitality for students and seniors, and these experiences promoted friendships and connections that continued outside of the classroom and many years into the future. Many of the seniors continued to correspond with the students as they moved through middle school and high school and beyond. When teachers create a classroom where everyone is welcome and appreciated for the unique gifts each brings, powerful learning can happen for everyone.

Discussion Questions

What would be your core beliefs that influence your definition of Christian hospitality in your classroom?

What are ways that you feel you could effectively unify all students in your classroom including those with special needs, disabilities, or other marginalized students?

Is it possible to act hospitably without kindness?

How do you model kindness in the classroom?

CONCLUSION

Of the many spiritual activities we do to enhance our nearness to God, giving and offering of self to another is one of the most powerful. Albert Schweitzer wrote, "At times our own light goes out and is rekindled by a spark from another person. Each of us has cause to think with deep gratitude of those who have lighted the flame within us" (www.brainyquote.com). An encounter grounded in love and given to another person may make a profound and lasting difference in the life of that individual. In a class of graduate students, I ask them to pretend they have to answer to a board of directors with twelve members made up of those who have influenced their life in positive ways. I ask each student to put names on chairs signifying those twelve board members. I have yet to have a student not mention one or more of their teachers who had powerful, lasting effects on their lives. We cannot discount the influence a teacher has on students, and we cannot deny that in turn, students may reach out and rekindle the light in others.

Jesus in his last words to His disciples gave them a charge, "But you will receive power when the Holy Spirit comes on you; and you will be my witnesses in Jerusalem, and in all Judea and Samaria, and to the ends of the earth" (Acts 1:8). When you throw a pebble in a pond, the circles emanate from its point of entry. When we reach out to others, they will also reach out to others still. Jesus calls us to reach out to those around us, then a little farther out, and then even farther still. Sharing hospitality begins in our own community and neighborhood and classrooms. The apostle Luke said, "From one man he made every nation of men, that they should inhabit the whole earth; and he determined the times set for them and the exact places where they should live" (Acts 17:26). God could have put you in any nation during any time. In accordance with His perfect plan, He chose for you to occupy this particular time in history, your particular vocation and people whose lives you will touch. He has a purpose for your life. When we become Christians, we are called ambassadors, or representatives, of Jesus Christ. When we share his love, kindness, hospitality, it's as though he is making his appeal to the world through us (2 Corinthians 5:20). As soon as each of us moved into our neighborhoods, our schools, our classrooms, Christ in you moved in there, too. Our honor and privilege is to be his official representatives of hospitality in our daily walk where we live and work.

I continue to grow in my understanding of what it means to trust in God and have faith in his promises. I find myself sometimes questioning God, saying, "I can't do this," or "Choose someone else who has better skills." Each time I am reminded of Moses stating the same argument, and God answering that He would do it for him. God reminds us to "Be still and know that I am God . . ." (Psalm 46:10). The stillness and patience he requires of all of us can sometimes be very challenging. He does not expect perfection. He just expects us to take the first step and to have faith in him to help us do the rest.

As teachers we are blessed in our vocation to have the opportunities to touch so many lives. I believe our challenge is to mediate the love of Christ to people, through the offer of hospitality, thus making a powerful statement to the world about who is interesting, valuable, and important. How will God use Christian hospitality in your classroom to make a difference in the successes of your students? The choices are yours to make.

Discussion Questions

Think about the people who have helped you build friendships
and extended hospitality in your life?

When you consider where you are in your life today, who can you
reach out to and extend hospitality?

Are there other ways to make hospitality a significant part of your
life? How can you take this ideal and make it your own?

Prayerfully consider how you will build hospitality at home,
in your community, and in your classroom.
What will this look like in each location?

REFERENCES

Anderson, D. W. (2011). Hospitable classrooms: Biblical hospitality and inclusive education. *Journal of Education & Christian Belief*, 15/1, 13–27.

Nouwen, H. J. M. (1975). *Reaching out: Three movements of the spiritual life*. New York: Image/Doubleday.

Palmer, P. (1998). *The courage to teach: Exploring the inner landscape of a teacher's life*. San Francisco: Jossey-Bass.

Webster, S. (1996). *Webster's new world dictionary and thesaurus*. New York: Hungry Minds.

5

Community

GARY TIFFIN

I HAVE ALWAYS LIVED and worked in community, both in my career in Christian higher education and always in a congregation. A few years ago my wife and I built our retirement home in a Christian retirement community. Support, assistance, accountability, deep fellowship, and numerous examples of justice, mercy, witness, and sacrifice have characterized all three of these community environments.

Many years ago, the Christian college where I taught faced a terrible and potentially destructive crisis, which threatened to permanently damage many years of progress and achievement. It centered in matters of trust, faith, and reputation of key members of that academic community. In the midst of this crisis, I more than once stated the following to those who cared to listen: "I did not join this academic community for money, prestige, or reputation—but for its mission and the joy of working with faculty, administration, and students in the fellowship of the pursuit of that mission. If that is taken away, there is no reason for me to remain."

This crisis made it much more difficult to carry out my daily tasks of class preparation, advising students, trusting colleagues, and retaining confidence in a promising future at the college. Students suffered in quiet and often unseen ways even as I suffered. A timely sabbatical for nine months, and wise guidance of the Board of Trustees, helped heal my heartache and an entire academic community threatened with implosion. I realized through this experience that a genuine sense of community provides the most essential foundation for fulfillment in any educational enterprise.

HEBREW ORIGINS

Our English word *community* derives from a similar Latin word that is rooted in corollary ideas of "together" and "with obligation" (Gereluk, 2006). Yet, the word *community* has multiple origins, both religious and secular. Several Hebrew words can be translated "community" as each has to do with gathering as an assembly to fulfill some purpose. In the Old Testament, the Israelites became a covenant community, primarily based upon their renewing of the Abrahamic Covenant and through the Law. This covenant provided promises and security for all Israel in return for obedience, faithfulness, and integrity. The key components of covenant keeping were faithfulness, lovingkindness, duty, and giving help to others, including God. We should view these today as prototype ingredients for "community keeping." These elements are often included in the larger discussion about community in education (Chickering, 2006). Covenant-keeping was best encapsulated in the Hebrew word *hesed*. For the Hebrew people, community directly related to survival in a desert, as they struggled to trust leaders, God, and each other for daily needs and facing an uncertain future. Their "choseness" was linked to their functioning as a revelatory community based upon God's direct plans and intention for them (and the world) as a people.

GREEK ORIGINS

The Greeks provided another part of our understanding of community from a very different context. While we might think of Greek society as secular, they did not separate the sacred and the secular as we are prone to do. That integration extended to the daily life of the city-state (*polis*) as well as their sense of connection to the Olympian Gods. Community for the Greeks was centered in the polis, which offered belonging, identity, purpose, and protection. These four benefits remain very significant components of the word *community* today. Community life (for Greek males only) was the vehicle of significance, achievement and meaning. Banishment (ostracism), not death, was the highest form of punishment for treason because the offender would suffer a fate worse than death, exile from the polis and thus the community offered by the city-state. It was a fate worse than death itself, and really was a form of death. In other words, life itself was understood within the context of community, outside of which there was no real life.

NEW TESTAMENT ORIGINS

The New Testament word for church is *ekklesia*, which means "called out ones." Even in the Old Testament, words for "congregation" were translated *ekklesia* or sometimes "synagogue" in the Septuagint translation from Hebrew to Greek completed well before the time of Christ. In Greek society, *ekklesia* referred to those who were "called out" from their normal routine to perform a particular service or duty for the polis, always for the benefit of the entire polis, the political community. This word eventually became the Biblical descriptor for communities of Christians (congregations) in the New Testament era. The New Testament transfers the Hebrew concept of *hesed* into new covenant terms that came to be understood, at the very least, as Christlikeness as a form of covenant keeping (New Covenant). So, deep within the historical origins of the Christian faith is this fundamental definition and description of congregational life as community. This signals that Christian community was intentional, purposeful, and transforming for all those involved.

The Christian concept of community is also defined by two Biblical words *hesed*, already discussed and *agape*. The Greek word, *agape*, is one of four Greek words for love. It defines how Christians are to function in community, as demonstrated by God as his disposition (*agape*) toward humanity in that very familiar verse in John 3:16. Agape love is to be differentiated from other Greek words for love such as *storge* (affection), *philos* (common bonds), and *eros* (obsessed with beauty and power). Agape signifies the intention to work for the best interests and success of the other. It creates value in the other, is not conditional or self centered and more importantly actually enhances the other three types of love already mentioned. A very compelling case can be made that the other three loves spoil and become destructive without the leavening influence of *agape*. For example, without the constraint of *agape*, *philos* tends to elevate and enable groups, such as nations, with a sense of superiority, which often takes the form of excessive nationalism. Without *agape*, *eros* often functions in self-centered and manipulative ways.

The metaphor of the "body" of Christ also contributes to the Christian concept of community, particularly as expressed by Paul in 1 Corinthians 12. There he outlines the functioning of the body as an organic whole, made up of many necessary parts that are intended to function in supportive harmony. In Acts 2 and 4, we see a worshipping and serving community of early Christians whose witness was expressed not only in the direct witness of the gospel message but also in their attending to each other's basic needs. Other New Testament metaphors hold community connotations, such as "bride of Christ," "vine and branches," "flock of God," "kingdom," and "temple or building" in the sense that such is composed of individual stones. Some historians, Stark (2011) in particular, contend that it was this sense of personal commitment to their own community of believers that was largely responsible for the early and quick spread of the Christian faith.

When the fundamental definitions of *hesed* and *agape* are integrated, the New Testament and Christian concept of community can be defined as "my voluntary and unconditional commitment to your success and best interests." This is then the culminating meaning of community that arose within the early Christian community. This very important component of our Christian heritage provides us with a model by which our pedagogy and relationships in educational communities can transform both our students and colleagues, from kindergarten through graduate studies in college. Examples of and ideas for this will be offered in this chapter.

COMMUNITY TODAY

For most of history, we were born into community. Until the industrial revolution, community was based upon an involuntary kinship-extended family system encompassing economic, political, social and religious sectors of life. In the last two centuries, the experience of community has transitioned toward communities based upon more artificial and transitory circumstances to the point that the great majority of us now live in an urbanized society featuring nuclear families (Gereluk, 2006). The nuclear family today, usually distanced from closest relatives such as grandparents, often further isolates members of the family unit.

Communities in general can and have historically functioned around any number of beliefs, needs, or exigencies. Current research and theory now include the concept of "shared intentionality" as a driving impulse to the formation of community (Haidt, 2012). The word *community* implies common bonds, common fate, common stakes, and some sense of collective identity and future. It certainly involves interdependence and integral linkage. They can be nothing more than a matter of geographical proximity—in the sense that the difference between a house and a home is not a matter of proximity. Community can be voluntary, forced, or simply expedient.

For the Christian educator, faith in Jesus brings us into community with God and others, as well as creation. We can enjoy, resist, or ignore any part of the many dimensions of community. This chapter presumes that we gladly receive and accept the sense of community offered by our faith and at the same time are seeking to fulfill its obligations as well as its promises. It is really about "community keeping," identified earlier in this introduction, which is driven by faithfulness, lovingkindness, duty, and giving help to others. In our educational environments we can ask for classroom observation from a colleague; bank sick leave for another instructor; refuse to believe a derisive report about another until the "facts" are clear, thus giving another the benefit of the doubt. We can also give and receive assistance for tasks simply too overwhelming for another colleague to accomplish. All this benefits students as we become more effective, open to help, and demonstrate interdependence rather than the destructive side of competitiveness. It should be noted that many teachers struggle with the high-stakes testing environment fostered by the implementation of the No Child Left Behind Act, which often pits teachers against each other and more often prevents teachers from giving adequate attention of differing learning styles of students, let alone their varying needs.

OUR CONTEXT AND SITUATION

Christian educators live and function in various types of communities. We live in geographical communities, work in educational communities, participate in worshipping communities, and can choose to participate in and enjoy a wide range of communities based upon mutual interests (hobbies, for example), civic groups, political concerns, etc. While we can view community in organizational and structural terms, this chapter will examine and analyze community in terms of how we function in relationships and how we sustain them, which is often missing in considering community.

In American education, we live with the challenges of our culture, as compared to many Eastern cultures, that emphasize, prize, and praise autonomy, self-reliance, rugged individualism, and personal rights. These ideals and traits have deeply defined and influenced each of us, both positively and negatively. Often it works against community by isolating and alienating us from each other. They tend to emphasize objects more than relationships. They can produce an overemphasis upon competition that blunts the cooperation essential to effective community. At the same time, we should embrace the upside of this aspect of American culture, prizing the independent thinker among us, giving serious consideration to "out-of-the-box" ideas. The paradox of allowing for independent thinking in a culture that highly values community is a challenge, but can become a rich part of community life in educational settings. I have been known to occasionally comment, in reference to a faculty member who could be difficult, sometimes aloof, but amazingly creative, that "I'm glad we have one of him, but one is enough."

Community does not require sameness, but embraces the rich diversity of personality, temperament, and disposition within the bounds of commitment to those who make up the community. Haidt (2012) has recently reminded us that community is built upon the presumption that we live and work best in recognition of our need for others, our willingness to subordinate our autonomy for the benefits of association, and that relationships ultimately define and propel us toward our best work and highest satisfaction.

Many have noted the loss of community in America over the last fifty years due to many factors, including our increasingly pluralistic population, the effects of one-issue politics, the so-called culture wars and increased personal mobility to name a few. This loss has resulted in increased alienation, depression, and anxiety in American society. Our challenge is to overcome these consequences of the waning of community as well as the power of the exaggerated cultural ideals of self-reliance and individualism, so we may express, enjoy, and live in community as understood from a biblical perspective. The rise of social media also challenges us to employ such for the building of genuine community through trust and authentic interactions.

An issue as divisive as immigration policy and governmental responses to the influx of illegal immigrants poses both a threat to educational communities, but also an opportunity. Too often we tend to disconnect from those with whom we disagree. How about collaborating with those holding very different views to create a forum or public discussion where all sides can speak and listen? My own experience in online instruction convinces me that even that medium holds great power for community building, but based upon new and very different presumptions and approaches. While we sometimes are teaching "strangers" which requires very careful communication, the same medium offers a wonderful venue for very careful, honest, and non-threatening learning moments.

PRACTICING AND SUSTAINING

In succeeding pages, the phrases "practice of community" and "sustaining community" will be used. These phrases need to be defined.

The practice of community refers to the actual living out of the definition and meaning of the word community, as earlier defined. So when we "practice community," we demonstrate our commitment to each other; we commit to fulfill our shared purpose(s); and we "have each other's backs" in terms of safety and protection. In short, *hesed*. This of course is an ideal, but a goal that when activated delivers great satisfaction and results, as envisioned by God for our benefit and the good of all with whom we are involved. If we really are our "brother's keeper," that can be expressed through an apology or willingness to receive an apology, asking for prayer or volunteering to pray, speaking in the defense of an accused or demeaned colleague, setting the record straight regarding an annoying student, disengaging from those speaking critical comments about a colleague when that colleague is not present, or balancing a legitimate casual complaint against an administrator in the faculty room—each of these illustrating the practice of community.

This takes dogged commitment and hard work, and is achieved gradually, not automatically. Review, assessment, and recalibration of our practices, communication and priorities are usually necessary to keep this "practice" alive and growing. This is the very essence of what this chapter is about, which leads us to the other half of the matter.

Sustaining community significantly undergirds the practice of community. If genuine community is to be experienced, enjoyed, celebrated and maintained, much effort (process) is required. It needs to be celebrated, evaluated, discussed, reviewed, modeled and taught. Certain contributing factors in the experience of community (such as giving the benefit of the doubt and gentle speech) require practice, repetition, and reminding, in order for it to take hold and display its benefits. Sustaining community results in a continuity of experience, which in turn reinforces its values and benefits. Regular and consistent protocols and evaluation points and continuous nourishment are required in sustaining community. Since we have already outlined all the forces in our culture that drag against community, we must almost overemphasize it, in order to sustain it. In this sense, community keeping is deeply rooted in covenant keeping which by definition is continuous, dynamic, and at times uncertain in its promise. For this reason, faculty retreats, special training sessions, and even special personal assistance preserve the benefits of any real community already attained.

Discussion Questions

How do you know if you are experiencing genuine community in your educational setting? Or if not?

Who is responsible for creating and sustaining community?

What is the basis for commitment to community among your non-Christian colleagues?

At what point do you know that community has been refreshed, initiated, or reset?

COMMUNITY IN EDUCATION

Educational settings are of course social institutions. Any consideration of community in education quickly moves beyond the obvious fact that education occurs in a geographical proximity that provides the obvious physical environment for community. Admittedly, with the growth of online education, community is no longer entirely dependent upon shared geographical space. Community in education is achieved intentionally, not naturally. Safe, loving, and considerate learning environments are fostered by community. Effective teaching is more likely when teachers feel supported and praised by peers and administrators. Students who are loved, appreciated, and held accountable become better prepared for real life and the accompanying opportunities and challenges. I was known as quite strict in setting deadlines in my undergraduate college world civilization courses. It usually took one or two "tests" of my policy for some students to actually believe I was serious. When questioned as to why I was so strict, my stock answer was, "the trains leave on time in England." Such an apparently silly answer soon became real when students understood that employers, medical personnel and life in general does not usually allow us to set our own schedules. My students knew I cared deeply about them, which helped them accept in theory what would someday be true in practice. In this sense, the classroom is a micro-community, a place to not only practice community, but also practice for life.

Taking time to give full feedback to students is a wonderful community gift. Most students would prefer a B grade with full written evaluation (even picky things like weak verbs and overuse of the passive voice) than an A grade without feedback. Our gift to our students is the gift of time and individualized effort, an extraordinary gift that comes within community.

The community in education that leads to the achievement of our goals centers on relationships, processes, attitudes, and collaborative working policies. Early education of children in America often took place in singular settings, with just a teacher and student(s). This did not last long, as the rapid growth of all levels of education into the twentieth century fostered complex organizations, multiple classrooms, administrative and support staff, as well as deep linkage to constituent communities for financial and policy support and input. The emerging interdependence of all facets of American education, at all levels, between families, towns, tax districts, and state/federal agencies is a fact of life today. Yet true community in education is not an automatic product of these several and separate structural components. Something more is needed. Commitment of effort and time, willingness to offer constructive appraisal and feedback, honest conversation, forgiveness, as well as grace and hospitality, as featured in two other chapters in this book, help define true community.

Community in education is not the special province of Christian educators. It is achievable by many means not necessarily rooted in Christian faith. Best practices in courtesy, group dynamics, curriculum formation and evaluation, professional development, and continuing education for teachers, while correlated to Christian principles and beliefs, are often shared and promoted by our colleagues who do not share our Christian faith. But that does not relieve Christian educators from the opportunity and obligation to lead, prompt, and collaborate towards effective community based upon our own sense of community originating from our Christian faith. For the sake of our students, as well as the credibility of our faith, we should strive to promote community as a key means by which effective education for our students is achieved. This can take many forms, from attending conferences together, committing to common planning time, and periodic shared meals. Hospitality and responses of grace should be commonplace in our lives, not just as a device for learning, but also as a context for every possible learning dynamic for our students.

Much of this is now occurring. Professional Learning Communities and a host of other cooperative and collaborative designs, such as mentoring, are increasingly common in formal educational settings. We now understand that how we learn is part of what we learn. It is clear that knowledge is no longer the private domain of the teacher or instructor—that our students and we study, probe, and learn together. The invitation to learn together is fundamental to learning in community. Giving help to others, especially our colleagues, is very important because it counters the downside of our tendency toward isolation, autonomy, self-reliance, individualism and fierce competitiveness. Examples of this are referenced earlier in this chapter.

Our attitudes toward support staff mirror the value of genuine community. If how I treat my mother is an accurate indicator of how I will treat my wife, then how I treat the "least" of school staff (cooks, janitors, various assistants, volunteers, etc.) is likely highly correlated to how and whether or not I can really practice community in the classroom. How about a surprise appreciation lunch, or arranging to end their day early and taking on their tasks? Lovingkindness and duty are then part of "community keeping". This really is a matter of how we view, value, and think about other human beings. Their value and potential (all theologically based in our Christian worldview) is at stake as we seek to implement the processes necessary to enjoy the fruit of community.

This is where the *hesed/agape* formulation connects to the Christian educator in the pursuit and practice of "community keeping." Christian educators should function from the motivating foundation and power of the Biblical concept(s) that generate, enhance, and form community. As already noted, other educators who responsibly participate in and promote community may function from a different value or pre-suppositional base. One does not have to be a Christian to act like one. But we must expect that Christian educators live out the defining characteristics inherent in cHesed and agape as earlier defined. When Paul urged us in Ephesians 5:15–16 to "redeem" the time, he was not only referring to witnessing to the message of redemption, but also to our opportunity and responsibility (faithfulness) to reclaim our own society and culture for God and benefit of all humanity, including the benefits of effective education. Ours is a stewardship of God's gifts to us and our own education as well as our personal experiences and opinions that we bring to our profession.

Ultimately, our participation in and promotion of community in education is about ministry. We each share the common and generic call to advance the mission of Christ, even through our profession. Ours then is the opportunity to live out our faith in the witness of promoting all the benefits of community in our own educational setting. Our worship (*latreo*—translated "service" in Romans 12:1) of God is as much about what we do in the workplace during the week, as it is about what we do on Sunday. It is a privilege and obligation to live out our calling through our career. This is usually accomplished through the quiet, applicable, competent, and appreciated contributions we make to colleagues and students in our leadership and participation in formal and informal educational settings. This can be expressed in a number of ways: including extra time spent, assisting beyond the call of duty, transferring sick time or vacation days, offering constructive feedback, or even appropriate and private suggestions for improvement.

Discussion Questions

What evidence of effective community in and/or
out of the classroom can you cite?

What hinders community in your school?

Can community be created and sustained by faculty
if not supported by administrators? Vice-versa?

COMMUNITY AND SERVICE

Many of us spend long hours at school, then some more grading and preparing in the evening, often in isolation from family, and then try to find time to participate in our church community. So we tend to segment our lives into distinct categories of work, home and church, forgetting or ignoring that the Christian life should be integrated into all aspects of society, culture, and our activity. So, even as the concept of community so far discussed has been described and promoted as internal to teaching and learning in school settings it also extends far beyond the school and classroom to our actual geographical settings. If community in education is so key and important for the best education of our students, it is then also applicable to other components of our social lives. It is generalizable to and intertwined with the educator's neighborhood, town or city, and even region or state. We recognize that the word community in this sense is a geographical concept. In fact, geographically based communities predated educational communities historically. At that, geography based community becomes the setting for another venue for both the practice of and sustaining of community. The recent trend toward "neighborhood" schools, ironically in the eyes of some, has resulted in the re-segregation of some communities, significantly reordering the nature of such communities.

The word service has origins in the Bible. It is synonymous with the Biblical word for ministry. It is also one of several Biblical words related to worship. This is best seen in Romans 12:1 where Paul used the phrase "your spiritual act of worship." Some versions of the Bible use the word *latreo* as "service" rather than "worship" in this verse. *Latreo* is one of the Greek words translated as "worship" in the New Testament. We can then conclude that any service or ministry we render in the locale where we live is an act of worship to/of God. This certainly elevates the bar relative to the importance of our activity beyond school and church, rising to the obligation of duty as part of "community keeping."

Let's return to Ephesians 5:15–16 where Paul urges that we "redeem" the time. While he certainly is referring to spiritual redemption (see his reference to "the days are evil" that follows), he is also including how we spend our time, life, and influence in our own community (town, city, place of residence). To redeem the time, to use our time wisely, or to make the most of every opportunity, is to reclaim our world for not only the sake of the gospel, but also for a quality of life worthy of God's purpose and intention for humanity and His creation. Therefore, activity on civic commissions, advisory committees, cultural affairs, and any elected office should be seen as an opportunity to "buy back" or redeem what is so easily lost in the life of a city, town, or region to violence, injustice, or apathy. It is to assist in recovering the decaying effects of a fallen world even as we await redemption. This is simply a matter of expressing solidarity with our own living communities. In other words, activity as described in this section promotes all the best features of community keeping based upon *hesed* and *agape*.

Meeting human need is certainly held up as an altruistic ideal outside of Christian settings. For Christians, responding to such needs through individual voluntary activity, group association or a formal role constitutes a vital part of our ministry (service) for Christ and the Christian community. Feeding the hungry, helping the poor, visiting the jailed, and clothing the naked exemplifies the very nature of Christ and the Christian community (see Matthew 25). Others may do it, but we Christians by the very nature of our commitment to Christ must be involved as an expression of our faith and love for our neighbors. When we help and care, people are enabled to believe God cares and can help. The role of educator in any locale (community) is enhanced, given credibility and highlighted by community service.

This service is not limited to what has been illustrated as community service so far. Our scholarship can also function as a vehicle of our service, depending upon our topic or purpose. Whether our scholarship privately informs our practice and effectiveness as an educator or is translated into articles, books, or public discourse, it ultimately serves the welfare of children, students and the purposes of education. Scholarship improves our competence and the credibility of our voice within our range of influence thus becoming another community asset.

Discussion Questions

Do you have time to promote community in your community?

What roles could you take on to promote community in your community?

Do you have time for this?

How could you apply your scholarship to help your community?

COMMUNITY OF FAITH

Christian educators usually define their lives largely in terms of their faith in Christ. Any discussion of a community of faith related to Christian educators begins with personal faith in terms of trust in Christ, spiritual disciplines, and evidencing of the fruit of the Spirit. But community of faith cannot be limited to the personal-individual sphere. The letters of Paul and others in the New Testament were written mostly to congregations, not to individuals. Christian faith and living is not an autonomous or private matter. It is lived out in public and in association with other Christians. Here again, we Americans are deeply influenced by our culture that prizes individualism, self-reliance, and "do it yourself" thinking. Images of body, saint, fellowship, etc., are found in the New Testament, underlining the interdependence of Christians in worship, witness, and the living out of their faith through activity, acts of mercy and justice, and service to others.

While association, fellowship, and interaction with other Christians in our schools are essential and laudable (particularly in public institutions), the idea of community of faith is fundamentally embedded in a local congregation. Membership or participation in a local congregation links us to other Christians outside of our profession. It also grounds us to the reality of many other walks of life, the needs of regular people, and how Christians together can meet local needs where they live. To the extent we educators are educated beyond the average church member, it is important that we practice humility, grounded in real life experience beyond the school or college and wary of intellectual arrogance. The elderly lady or man, the poor family, the single father, the abused orphan or the teen who needs a mentor—each in their own way—reminds us constantly of real human need and why/how the gospel links to all of life including our ministry through education. We could take on non-professional roles related to congregational life, such as working the food bank, yard work, medical transportation, or janitorial duties.

The prayers of our colleagues, sharing the joys and frustrations of our professional work with other educators, and fellowship with others in our field about issues we face daily are important and help sustain us. But the continuous fellowship, accountability, corporate worship, and collective witness available only in congregational life are even more important. Congregations were ordained by God, as his instrument to carry out his will. It is part of the manifestation of Christ termed as the body of Christ. If Christ is the head of the church (Ephesians 1), then we cannot and should not deny our intended relationships with other brothers and sisters in Christ. They were never intended to be random, casual, selective or periodic. They are intended as continuous, sustaining, organic, and essential to our lives and witness.

Our options for expressing and engaging in Christian community are several. We can teach, serve as a church officer, volunteer for social outreach programs (food bank, after school programs, etc.) support with our tithes and offerings, offer ourselves to others in our regular attendance and involvement in worship, programs, and activities which produce credibility and witness through the sphere of influence of our local congregation. Our faithful involvement in our local congregation turns out to be a witness in itself to other colleagues and our students in our professional setting. People know—it does not have to be broadcast, just simply lived.

Discussion Questions

Are you viewed as a contributing member
of your religious community?

Some would disagree with the ideal that we must be active
in a local congregation. Why or why not?

In what ways can your educational activity, role(s) and profession
contribute to the work, ministry, and success of your congregation?

CONCLUSION

We were created for community and actually live, work, and function best in healthy community environments. We believe this not just because of experience, formal studies, or even intuition, but because community is rooted in our Christian faith and Biblical tradition. As Christian professional educators, we fulfill our personal, professional, and religious calling much more effectively and joyfully as we recognize and live out the rich meaning of community in every phase of our lives. It is in our DNA awaiting activation through its practice and processing.

REFERENCES

Chickering, A. (2006). *Encouraging authenticity and spirituality in higher education*. San Francisco: Jossey-Bass.

Gereluk, D. (2006). *Education and community*. London: Continuum.

Haidt, J. (2012). *The righteous mind: Why good people are divided by politics and religion*. New York: Pantheon.

Stark, R. (2011). *The triumph of Christianity: How the Jesus movement became the world's largest religion*. New York: HarperCollins.

6

Care

GARY M. KILBURG

> A new commandment I give to you, that you love one another: just as I have loved you, you also are to love one another. By this all people will know that you are my disciples, if you have love for one another. (John 13:34–35, ESV)

IN THE BEGINNING . . .

JACK WILLIAMS, MY HIGH school choir director, was one of the most influential teachers I have ever known and was responsible for teaching me that my best was better than I thought. He had a caring heart and a willingness to invest in his students' lives. Mr. Williams was not just a teacher; he was an architect of souls. He didn't just teach students about the joy of music and preparing for a performance, he taught us about discipline, commitment, working together as a team, and trust. His love of God, his family, life, music, and his students was something that I have never forgotten. Even today, after forty-three years of teaching, I continue to practice those valuable life skills he taught me.

Students could always count on Mr. Williams for a positive attitude and spirit to guide and direct the choir. On those occasions when choir members needed correction, he was more than willing to confront in a loving way and help us understand the value of correcting our behavior. He rarely provided us with a solution to a problem. He helped us understand the value of making good choices based on the best interest of the individual and choir.

Mr. Williams provided students with consistency and boundaries. He knew that some of his students in choir did not have much of a home life with consistency and boundaries as a norm. He created a few concise and fair boundaries for his classes. We always knew where we stood in his classes and he never seemed to favor one student over another, which earned him the respect of his students.

He also provided many opportunities for students to experience success in choir, whether as a soloist or section leader. He acted as an instrument of inspiration and a witness for the potential in everyone. I clearly remember during my freshman year when Mr. Williams asked me if I would be interested in singing in a folk group. Hesitant at first, I agreed only after he and several of my friends talked to me a little more. Little did I know how much my life would change from that point on.

Over the next three-and-one-half years our singing group, the Folk Williams Four Plus One, performed at many venues, including colleges and local state and regional conferences. We cut a record during our senior year. This amazing ride started with Mr. Williams and his vision that involved a few young men. He remained committed to helping us succeed and provided numerous opportunities for growth while taking a back seat so that we could shine.

Many years have passed since I graduated from high school and I still remember what Mr. Williams did for me. I am forever grateful for his commitment and belief in me. The last time I saw Mr. Williams was his picture at his funeral several years ago. The hundreds of former students, family, and friends attending the memorial served as evidence of the high regard we all had for our teacher and friend. As a tribute to Mr. Williams, students from the past thirty years sang the *Hallelujah Chorus*, one of his favorite pieces of music. As I listened to the choir, I could just see Mr. Williams smiling from above and I could not help but remember the wonderful memories that I had of Mr. Williams and his love of music, his students, and his willingness to walk the extra mile for all of us. Mr. Williams continues to serve as an inspiration to me because of the love he had for his craft and for his students. His investment in his students really had nothing to do with making him look good as a choir director or teacher. It did, however, have everything to do with helping students understand that their best was better than they thought it was.

Mr. Williams' life demonstrates what a philosophy of care can do for students. This chapter will examine some of the factors that Mr. Williams and other effective teachers have demonstrated in creating an environment where a caring heart is commonplace. Those factors include:

- Bringing out the best in students

- Building trust

- Upholding positive expectations and purpose

- Creating boundaries for students

- Confronting with care

- Caring for self

BRINGING OUT THE BEST IN STUDENTS

"Each one should use whatever gift he has received to serve others, faithfully administering God's grace in its various forms." (1 Peter 4:10)

Teaching involves much more than just teaching about the subject. Caring teachers invest in the lives of students, and put forth every effort to increase their quality of life, just like Jesus did for us. Unfortunately, some teachers are technically smart, but human relations "dumb." They may have all the right answers for the subject and grade level they teach, but they are unaware that simply knowing information does not lead to effective and successful teaching. In other words, they do not appear to care.

Glasser (1992) believes that although quality may be difficult to define precisely, it almost always includes care for one another, it is useful, it involves hard work, and it produces a good feeling for those involved. Glasser's description identifies those schools and/or teachers that provide a caring and quality environment beyond the job description. Barkley (2005), relates a story of one teacher's efforts at creating a quality environment for her special-education students at the beginning of the year.

A special-education teacher in Georgia learned her class would be held that year in a portable trailer. The first day of school she dressed with curlers in her hair, slippers on her feet, and licorice on her teeth to look like they were missing—making the point they were located in a trailer, away from the main school building. After a few minutes of students gawking at her, she disrobed and underneath had on a beautiful sequined dress, high heels, and classy jewelry. She told the children that their trailer was like Cinderella's magic pumpkin. All sorts of magic occurred there, and they were going to have year of wonderful full of magical surprises. (p. 13)

This story is an illustration of how one teacher made a difference. She was committed to caring for her students throughout the school year and helping them to see that their best was better than they thought it was. There are a lot of things that this teacher could be known for, but the only thing that mattered to her was the investment that she wanted to make in her student's lives.

Aside from providing a quality environment, the simplest way to bring out the best in our students involves maintaining a value added perspective. Instead of looking for missing skills or abilities, we need to re-frame our expectations to look for the positive. If we make a conscious choice to expect the best from others, we will more than likely get it. In the end, behavior toward students, genuinely expressed, will begin to create the self-fulfilling prophecy that students are more than they seem from the outside (Covey, 2006).

Discussion Questions

What are the ways in which you try to bring out the best in people with whom you serve, work, and play?

How do you plan to bring out the best in your students?

Helpful Hints

You and I have an assignment from God. We should always be encouraging and improving someone else's life.

Always try to sow seeds of greatness in each person that you encounter.

BUILDING TRUST

"...let us not love with words or tongue but with actions and in truth." (1 John 3:18)

Caring teachers begin building trust the first day of class. Teachers must earn trust; it is not an entitlement. Students who trust teachers will become their advocates. Brooks and Brooks (2008) support the belief that:

> Students will come to trust teachers for the same reasons. They will come to trust you if they feel safe spiritually, physically, socially and mentally/emotionally in your classroom. Students who know you care about them will trust you. Students who know that you are reliable and consistent will trust you. Students who get academic and personal help from you when they make mistakes will trust you. (p. 2)

In every relationship—personal and professional—what the teacher does has far greater impact than anything the teacher says. But unless behavior demonstrates sincerity, words will not build trust; in fact, they will destroy it.

The process of teaching represents the process of fulfilling commitments made to students and to the school. Caring teachers understand that they must assume a posture of indebtedness because all students have a right to ask many things of their teacher. The answers to the questions below are some of the promises that teachers make. Coincidentally, they are also questions educators would ask of other instructors who teach them, and caring teachers are able to respond affirmatively to each of them:

Can I trust you to anticipate my needs?

Can I trust you to demonstrate that you care for me?

Can I trust you to act reliably and consistently?

Can I trust you to help me correct my mistakes and help me learn from them?

Can I trust you to help me feel competent and successful?

Creating a trusting environment means that we care enough to treat every student respectfully and equally. Students recognize inequality, and inconsistency can lead to distrust and can discourage a freedom of sharing within the classroom. When students learn in an environment where everyone receives equal treatment, students will feel safe and open to working with the teacher and with their peers.

Caring teachers keep their word. From returning graded papers on time to responding to concerns that students may be facing in school, educators who build trust stay true to that promised to students. Students also learn to trust teachers who act with integrity and consistency. When trusted teachers make mistakes, they admit it. An apology goes a long way with students. When teachers act and respond with honesty and humility, teachers can expect a high-trust environment. Teachers who are open to admitting mistakes have students willing to take risks, themselves.

Finally, encourage students to speak up if they don't understand a topic or the task at hand and work with them until they do. Regardless of how often the teacher explains or models the content covered, the teacher's willingness to promote learning elevates the level of trust in the classroom and is critical to the learning environment.

Discussion Questions

Why should students trust you?

In what ways have you prepared yourself to be a trustworthy person?

How are you planning on creating a high-trust environment in your classroom?

Helpful Hints

You cannot truly listen to anyone and do anything else at the same time.

Your body language needs to be congruent with what you say.

Do not promise what you can't deliver.

There is no excuse for rude behavior on the part of the teacher.

UPHOLDING POSITIVE EXPECTATIONS AND PURPOSE

"Be completely humble and gentle; be patient, bearing with one another in love. Make every effort to keep the unity of the Spirit through the bond of peace." (Ephesians 4:2)

A teacher's attitude and actions leave lasting impressions. Effective and caring teachers recognize that everyone experiences discouragement and depression, but they also realize that students have a choice in how to respond to setbacks. Self-defeating thoughts and self-imposed ceilings limit progress while positive thoughts and attitudes determine success. Those who have no strength to overcome negative mind-sets fail to reach the potential God intended. A barrier that resides inside the mind, rather than a lack of resources or a shortage of talent, prevents success.

Jesus was very clear about how we need to deal with self-defeating thoughts and limits. He told us that in this life we would have trouble but we would overcome (John 16:33). He was not saying that troublesome times would not come; He was saying that when they do, we can choose our attitudes. One of my favorite stories comes from the writing of Osteen (2004), because it illustrates how a boy chose a positive attitude.

> A little boy went out to the backyard to play with a baseball and bat. He said to himself, "I am the best hitter in the world." Then he threw the ball up in the air and took a swing at it, but he missed. Without a moment's hesitation, he picked the ball up again, saying as he swung the bat, "I'm the best hitter in all the world." He swung and missed, Strike two. He tossed the ball up in the air for a third time, concentrating more intensely, and even more determined, saying, "I am the best hitter in all the world!" He swung the bat with all his might. WHIFF! Strike three. The little boy laid his bat down on the ground, smiled real big. "What do you know?" He said. "I'm the best pitcher in the world!" (p. 113)

That child displayed a positive attitude. Teachers who care make attempts to develop positive attitudes in their students regardless of the circumstances from which their students come. Whether life is a privilege or pain has nothing to do with the circumstances of our lives; however, it is direct reflection of our attitudes. As difficult and as painful, and as unpredictable as life can be, it cannot defeat you unless you choose to be defeated. Caring teachers recognize opportunities to help students develop positive attitudes and they know those attitudes can determine the success or failure of a student.

Caring and effective teachers expect their students to make mistakes, and rather than criticizing, they recognize the importance of teaching students how to cope with their failures and learn from them. All educators should strive to create an environment where failure does not become fatal and does not defeat enthusiasm. A caring attitude prompts teachers to help students learn that the way people deal with things that go wrong is an indicator of the type of choices students make and how they deal with change.

Too often we make the choice to avoid a particular situation or activity because it makes us feel uncomfortable. An example of this can be found in McNally's (1990) book that talks about the Oscar-winning movie, *Chariots of Fire*. The actor playing the British Olympic champion Harold Abraham; declares after losing a race, "I run to win, and if I can't win, I won't run." The response from his friend brings Abrahams back to reality that we all face: "If you don't run, you can't win." There is good reason not to quit. Losing, like winning, is a habit. The best teachers expect their students to make mistakes, and then they teach the students to cope with failures and learn through an attitude of hope.

As stated in the chapter on Joy, attitudes toward the challenges in our classrooms affect our joy. In addition to joy, living with purpose and a positive attitude, allows us to take charge of our lives in ways that have profound consequences—on us and on our students. We must model for students that having purpose in our lives is not a panacea for happiness or perpetual good feelings. Positive expectations and purpose do, however, provide the solid foundation for all other perspectives on happenstance and that makes life worth living, no matter how grave the challenges. Every student deserves such lessons in life.

Discussion Questions

What is the attitude that you bring to work?

How will you model a positive attitude with the people you work with and your students?

> **Helpful Hints**
>
> Helping others can reduce stress in your own life.
>
> Surround yourself with colleagues and friends that have healthy and positive attitude.
>
> Smile.

CREATING BOUNDARIES FOR STUDENTS

"I will instruct you and teach you in the way you should go; I will counsel you and watch over you." (Psalms 32: 8)

No classroom, family, or individual can function without boundaries or clearly understanding expectations. Safety limits are nonnegotiable. By setting limits for students, teachers help them become responsible and accountable for their actions and help them learn to set limits for themselves. Other rules for behavior may emerge as a set of mutually agreed upon standards, but regardless of whether limits are unilaterally set or democratically constructed, all students benefit from clearly defined expectations and boundaries.

Students should not have to guess if they need to raise hands during a question and answer period nor should they need to interpret subtle signals to determine what the teacher wants them to do. From the very first day of school, teachers need to teach and review the various expectations and classroom procedures. Leinhardt, Weidman, and Hammond (1987) found that effective teachers spend more time during the first four days of school on management tasks than on academic tasks. Bluestein (2011) suggests that we all need a combination of structure (boundaries/expectations) and autonomy (power and control) in our lives. A lot of the defiance, rebelliousness, and acting out that occurs in the classroom reflect our students' struggle to survive. When teachers set boundaries and offer choices, and follow through consistently when boundaries have been violated, it creates a positive environment that reduces conflict, increases cooperation, and provides a caring and emotionally safe classroom.

The following checklist, adapted from Bluestein's (2011) work, can help new teachers determine whether or not their classroom contributes to an emotionally safe environment for students. Increasing the level of agreement with any of the bulleted items and the teacher will likely produce improvements in learning, on-task behavior, commitment, cooperation, and student responsibility. To check your own ability to create a caring classroom, decide if you always, sometimes, rarely, or never agree with the following:

- I sometimes allow students to create, design, or negotiate assignments to make them personally meaningful.

- I motivate through access to positive outcomes, rather than avoidance of fear of negative outcomes.

- I emphasize the positive consequences of cooperation.

- I consciously anticipate what students, teachers, and parents will need in various situations in order to prevent problems from occurring.

- I follow through immediately, avoiding warnings and threats.

- I make students and their parents aware of changes in behavior or performance that could affect grades or promotion.

Setting boundaries not only sends a message of care to students, it shapes the classroom environment. "They are intended to help students accomplish a particular task, rather than prevent inappropriate behavior as in the case of rules" (Burden, 2003, p. 86). Boundaries structure direct activities such as coming in from recess, handing in completed work, using the restroom, picking up graded papers, working in groups, or preparing for the beginning and end of class. According to Burden, the use of these procedures or routines has several advantages: "they increase the shared understanding of an activity between the teacher and students, reduce the complexity of the classroom environment to a predictable structure, and allow for efficient use of time" (p. 86). All in all, boundaries set up opportunities for success in student behavior and reflect care on the part of the teacher.

When determining the appropriate and effective procedures, decide specifically what routines and procedures are needed for a structured, but student-friendly classroom. In establishing routines and procedures, ensure that students understand the reason for the routine and/or procedure. Effective teachers create an ethos of care when modeling the procedure because they demonstrate their desire for students to do these things well. Then, they provide opportunities for students to model routines. Overwhelming students with a large number of routines and procedures will only serve to confuse and frustrate. Establishing routine takes time and bears repeating in order for them to become a natural part of student behavior.

Whatever message you intend to communicate, make sure that verbal and nonverbal messages are consistent. When messages are inconsistent, the listener becomes confused. Inconsistency can also create a lack of trust and undermine the chance to build a good working relationship with the student, and thus work against a culture of care.

Discussion Question

What boundaries are you going to set in your classroom and what are the consequences for students that step over the boundaries?

Helpful Hints

The purpose of boundaries is to teach, not to punish.

Boundaries offer choices with consequence.

Setting boundaries is not the same as issuing an ultimatum.

CONFRONT WITH CARE

"Let us therefore make every effort to do what leads to peace and to mutual edification." (Romans 14:19)

Conflict typically represents a struggle between and among students and teachers over beliefs, status, power, or resources. When we view conflict as a normal and inevitable part of school life, we are less likely to see it as a contest to create winners and losers. When conflict is acknowledged, accepted, and managed in an effort to restore balance and harmony in the classroom, confrontation becomes a win-win situation for students and teacher.

Conflict on the job sometimes gets out of hand because we care too much. In our desire to avoid hurting someone's feelings, we allow the problem to escalate out of control without confronting the issue. Teachers have a responsibility to confront a student when that person threatens the health and safety of another student, disrupts the educational process, or causes property loss or damage.

Teachers and students must learn and practice the art of caring confrontation on a daily basis. While confrontation can cause discomfort, Augsberger (2009) suggests several important guidelines for confrontation that include the expression of genuine concern, calm and tactful conversation, clear communication about desired outcomes, acknowledgment of the intentions of the person, and an objective account of the observed behavior. In addition to Augsberger's suggestions, I recommend avoiding power struggles, maintaining neutral body language, focusing on changing behavior rather than punishment, and separating negative comments from the issue at hand. The objective of confrontation remains grounded in the caring desire to change and shape behavior.

Teachers new to the profession wanting ways to respond to inappropriate behavior may want to consider several programs used in schools. They include, but are not limited to the following:

- Love and Logic©—This method of working with students focuses on modifying inappropriate behavior by making responsible choices. Information for this method can be found at www.loveandlogic.com.

- Courageous Conversations©—This time, subject and age dependent model responds to a specific type of conflict. Confronting problems though conversation in the classroom leads to change. Ten questions that help guide the conversation can be found at www.courageousconversations.net.

- Peer Mediation—This negotiation-based strategy teaches students to be mediators and provides the students with alternative strategies to resolve conflict among peers. In peer mediation, students trained as conflict managers apply problem-solving strategies to assist their peers in settling disputes in a manner satisfying to all parties. Information regarding this model can be located at www.indiana .edu/~safeschl/PeerMediation.pdf and http://cecp.air.org/ preventionstrategies/conflict.htm.

- Group Problem Solving—The classroom teacher can use group problem solving processes such as classroom meetings when dealing with conflicts or difficulties affecting the entire class. Classroom meetings provide a time for the entire class of students to discuss their concerns and work towards resolution. Additional information on this problem solving process can be found at www.cls.utk.edu/pdf/ls/Week3_Lesson21.pdf.

- Breaking Down the Walls©—All students need to accept and understand other cultures in the diverse world in which we live. This program invites everyone to become involved in finding common ground with the people we come into contact with without being judgmental. This program provides both teachers and students with an opportunity to examine their own belief system and the impact that has on the people. This program is located at library.thinkquest.org/CRO0212302.

- Natural Helpers©—This program, appropriate for students mainly in the middle and secondary schools, helps young people develop knowledge and skills in problem solving, and thus positively impact other students and the school. Information regarding this program can be found at www.be.wednet.edu/OurSchools/hs/clubs/natural_helpers/goals.htm.

Finally, administrators and teachers can also integrate conflict resolution into the school through the curriculum. Real world conflict necessitates the provision of opportunities for students to learn about conflict resolution as a part of the curriculum. Some suggested teaching strategies include: case studies, debates, panel discussions, mock trials, game shows, questioning strategies, reflective thinking, using class meeting as a method of conflict resolution and working peer criticism into writing instruction. The following resources illustrate ways to integrate conflict resolution into the curriculum:

- www.lessonplanet.com. This website search engine provides hundreds of lesson plans for K-12 that includes conflict resolution. The website requires a small fee per year for use of the materials, but many find the content worth the price.

- www.teachervision.fen.com/interpersonal-skills/resource/55817.html. Help students develop interpersonal skills with printed resources, activities, and lesson plans. Lessons include such topics as conflict, friendship, equality and peace.

- www.cccoe.net/social/skillslist.htm. This website provides teachers with lesson plans on a variety of skills that relate to conflict resolution for middle school students.

- www.pbs.org/teachers/search/resources/?q=conflict+resolution&x =38&y=13. This website offers 52 lessons on conflict resolution for K-12 schools in a variety of subjects.

- www.educationworld.com/a_lesson/. Teachers can find articles and lessons relating to conflict resolution in K-12 schools.

- www.responsiveclassroom.org/resourcessearch?search=conflict+res olution&term_node_tid_depth=All. This site has articles and blogs that are helpful for the classroom teacher.

- www.teachersnetwork.org/lessonplans/. Teachers Network seeks to improve student learning by helping teachers integrate web-based lessons into their instructional practice.

Caring confrontation for the purpose of helping students behave appropriately reflects love for students. A willingness to help students become better decision makers in the real world demonstrates a caring disposition. When we care enough to confront, we recognize the potential for growth not only in our students, but in ourselves as well.

Discussion Questions

Are you able to manage conflict with another person easily?

How are you preparing yourself to deal with conflict that may occur in the classroom?

Helpful Hints

Safety issues are non-negotiable.

Don't get involved with power struggles.

Learn to neutralize arguments.

Don't threaten, plead, or nag your students, because students typically
see this as a sign of weakness on the part of the teacher
and some students will take advantage of that.

If you are incorrect about something you said,
be accountable and apologize.

CARING FOR SELF

"For it is God who works in you to will and to act according to his good purpose."
(Philippians 2:13)

Creating a school environment that supports and nurtures teachers requires hard work. The organizational structures of many schools do not sustain the fellowship needed among faculty (Farber, 2010; Fullan, 2001; Nieto, 2003). Unfortunately, the lack of fellowship and contact with other professionals leaves many teachers, including those new to the profession, to solve their own problems. Fortunately, new and veteran teachers can take charge of their own professional growth by building a support network that breaks through the isolation that many teachers experience. For some teachers, a support network may mean having access to and discussing curriculum resources. Another teacher may require weekly meetings with a mentor. Others may require help with a behavioral problem, or upcoming parent conferences.

Whatever path teachers choose to take to create support networks, proactive efforts will result in greater self-care. Support networks allow teachers to know the people in the various departments, grade levels, and specialties. In one case, a teacher new to the district made a point of bringing a plate of cookies to the first meeting of the school year and began to make connections that way. Another teacher sat at a different table at every staff meeting. Isolation in the workplace can lead to indifference—the antithesis of care.

Many schools reduce the isolation of teachers through mentoring programs. Teachers in schools without mentoring programs should seek out a trusted veteran as a mentor. A school culture that invites and supports caring collaboration can expect a cohesive and effective staff. All teachers might wish to take time to determine which colleagues would likely provide support, and then ask if the person might willingly provide time to mentor. Those who choose to mentor often find that they benefit professionally from the relationships. Self-care can involve giving to others through service in the form of a mentorship.

Self-care demands separation from the club of teachers who whine and moan about almost everything. These unprofessional educators suck the life out of their colleagues who attempt to advance their practice and the quality of the learning environment (Barth, 2006). Once people become members of this club, peer pressure and agreement keep them locked in the clubhouse because the toxic attitudes become a way of life (Barkley, 2005). Strong teachers make every effort to avoid these negative elements in the school. The lack of enthusiasm for teaching on the part of those in the club can permeate throughout a school at a rapid pace and alienate those who have not forgotten the joy in teaching expressed in the chapter by Birky.

We can practice self care by making an effort to connect with experienced teachers who enjoy their work, engage in ongoing professional development activities, and who are enthusiastic about their teaching. Teachers can also create a professional and fellowship network by forming or join a support group with other teachers in the district. Establishing a peer group provides teachers with a safe place to exchange ideas and discuss common issues. The group can also provide emotional support for those times when challenges occur.

Self-care may come easily for those with a good sense of humor. We have all known the classic tight-jawed sourpuss who takes everything with deathly seriousness and rarely laughs at anything. Teachers should not take themselves so seriously that they never feel good about the work they do. Laughter is a powerful antidote for stress, pain, and conflict. Nothing works faster or more dependably than a laugh to bring balance and joy into our lives and work.

Humor lightens burdens, connects people, keeps us grounded, and demonstrates humility.

I remember one night I received a phone call about 1:45 am. As I staggered out of the bedroom, I ran into the wall and after finally figuring out where the phone was, I picked it up and said, "Hello." The voice on the other end of the line said, "Good evening, Mr. Kilburg. We are having a problem with your telephone service and we were wondering if you would mind checking it for us?" Still half asleep, and without giving it a second thought, I said, "Sure." The next thing the voice asked me to do was to sing *Old McDonald Had a Farm*, so that they could check the phone line to see if it was working. Without hesitation and still groggy, I began to sing. After I completed the song, I could hear muffled laughter in the background and the voice thanked me for helping them out. I asked them if they needed me to sing any more, but the response was, "No, thank you, you've done enough already." I hung up the phone and as I began walking back to my bed, it finally dawned on me that someone had played a good practical joke on me. I crawled back in bed, but couldn't get to sleep. All I could think about was how goofy I sounded and that just cracked me up. Later, I thought it would be fun to share my little adventure with my students. So at the beginning of class I took the first 5 minutes to tell my students about my Old McDonald Farm adventure and my students loved it. I wasn't just a teacher, I was also a human being that wasn't afraid to laugh at himself when he made a mistake, and that is something the students appreciated.

Humor can allow us to see that we are not perfect, and laughing at ourselves demonstrates our humility. Recognizing the need for laughter in our lives adds to the self-care we all need to experience. It helps to reduce the seriousness that can saturate the educational environment. Maybe if we develop a willingness and ability to laugh at ourselves more often, students will begin to develop some of the same strategies that will help them navigate life's bumpy road.

Discussion Questions

What do you do to relax?

Do you have a trusted friend that you can talk too?

When do you laugh?

> **Helpful Hints**
>
> Make time for daily devotions and prayer.
>
> Exercise regularly and create regular opportunities for downtime.
>
> Spend time with people that have a positive outlook on life
> and are willing to help others.

IN CONCLUSION . . .

Mr. Williams knew that having purpose in his life was really about bringing out the best in the students and adults with whom he worked. He understood that God continually looks for ways to help improve people's lives and we should expect the same for one another. Instead of performing post mortems on the failures of his students, Mr. Williams took the high road and looked for strengths that others might have overlooked. The way we live our lives should inspire others to do better, and Mr. Williams did that on a daily basis. His legacy of care served as a testimony to the trusting environment that he created for his students. In the end, Mr. Williams knew that the only thing that really mattered was the investment we make in one another's lives.

I will be forever grateful for Mr. Williams' positive influence and his commitment and willingness to teach me that my best was better than I thought it was.

REFERENCES

ATI. (2011, March 31). *Courageous conversations: Resolve conflicts through clear communication*. Retrieved March 2, 2011 from http://ati.iblp.org/ati/family/articles/concepts/courageousconversations/.

Augsberger, D. (2009). *Caring enough to confront*. Ventura, CA: Regal.

Barkley, S. G. (2005). *Quality teaching in a culture of coaching*. New York: Rowman & Littlefield Education.

Barth, R. S. (March 2006). Improving relationships within the schoolhouse, *Educational Leadership, 63*, (6), 8–13.

Bluestein, J. (2/24/2011) *Creating a caring classroom*. Retrieved February, 24, 2011 from http://www2.scholastic.com/browse/article.jsp?id=4428.

Burden, P. R. (2003). *Class-room management: Creating a successful learning community*. New York: Wiley.

Covey, S. M. R. (2006). *The speed of trust: The one thing that changes everything.* New York: Free Press.

Eiseley, L. (1978). *The star thrower.* New York: Harvest Books.

Fullan, M. (2004). *Leading in a culture of change.* San Francisco, CA: Jossey-Bass.

Glasser, W. (1992). Quality, trust, and redefining education. *Education Week,* 5/13/92.

Leinhardt, G., Weidman, C., & Hammond. K.M. (1987). Introduction and integration of classroom routines by expert teachers. *Curriculum Inquiry,* 17(2), 135–176.

McDonnell. Retrieved from http://www.ascd.org/publications/educational-leadership/ summer09. (2011, February 9). Re: *The Last of the Human Freedoms: Acts* 16: 22–34 [Online sermon]. Retrieved from http://firstpresfwb.org/May_28_sermon.pdf.

McDonnell, S. N. (2009, July). The art of caring confrontation. *Educational Leadership,* 66. Retrieved June 6, 2011, from http://www.ascd.org/publications/educational-leadership/summer09/.

McNally, D. (1990). *Even eagles need a push: Learning to soar in a changing world.* Eden Prairie, MI: Transform Press.

Nieto, S. (2003). *What keeps teachers going?* New York: Teachers College Press.

Osteen, J. (2004). *Your best life now: 7 steps to living at your full potential.* NewYork: Warner Faith.

Wong, H. K., & Wong, R. T. (2001). *How to be an effective teacher: The first days of school.* Mt. View, CA: Wong.

7

Wonder

KEN BADLEY

FOR DECADES, I HAVE hiked in the Rocky Mountains of western Canada. On one such hike, the three men with me and I froze in our tracks, single file, when we surprised a ptarmigan next to our trail. This member of the grouse family, who enjoys good camouflage, never flinched while the four of us kept our gaze from a few meters away. We—that is both parties—held our positions for about two minutes, the hikers in a state of wonder, and the bird . . . I cannot guess. By wonder, I mean that we were silent, amazed, and in awe. We were attending fully to the bird and were quite unaware of the passage of time, the weight of our packs, our shortage of breath, or the burning sensation in our legs. Some would say we were childlike.

As it happens, the ptarmigan needs good camouflage because of a widely reputed shortage of intelligence; he is no crow when it comes to cognition. On that occasion, I had the last position in our group and therefore had in my field of vision not just the bird but also my three companions. I would love to claim that we stood enraptured by this bird for the rest of the afternoon. I do not recall who spoke first or if anyone spoke at all. But my own humbling epiphany came when I realized that a bird—there is no more appropriate adjective than a *stupid* bird—had the power to stop in our tracks four adults, all of us called "doctor" at our respective medical and academic workplaces. Our collective IQ was well beyond that of the bird in front of us. This dramatic contrast of intelligence levels produced my epiphany and the humility that followed.

In narrating my friends' and my encounter with the ptarmigan, I am trying to persuade you and perhaps myself of what artists and poets have called and invited us to do for generations: to live in wonder. As busy educators, we can easily get mired down in the details of curriculum, planning, assessment, and the myriad other administrative details of our work. But I want to invite us in this chapter to (re)discover the artists' and poets' invitation to live in wonder. And I want to invite us to think about our curriculum, planning, and instruction in ways that invite our students to do the same.

We have all had similar experiences in nature to the one I described above. Some of us have seen the Milky Way, perhaps on a thousand different pitch-black nights. Some have seen the aurora borealis or northern lights. Some have hiked, peddled, climbed, and paddled to natural places that took our breath away, usually in wonder but probably sometimes in fear. Extremes of weather and the power of that weather can reduce us to wonder. As some poets have told us, the world is alive with God's splendor. And for many of us that splendor produces wonder.

But there are other sources of wonder. Human actions and products also may cause us to wonder. In galleries, I have stood in awe of the abilities of artists and the gifts of beauty they have given us all. As have you, I have heard great music, not only from Bach and Rodriguez but from Diana Krall and Eric Clapton. Great buildings have elevated my eyes and thoughts, while increasing my admiration for those who designed and built them. Fyodor Dostoevsky and Flannery O'Connor have troubled me with their words. Dorothy Sayers and Woody Allen have used theirs to make me cry and laugh and wonder. I stand in awe of and in debt to these and many other writers. How can one not wonder—and I do not mean about plagiarism—when a student writes an outstanding paper or even a great sentence? And how can one not wonder when someone sends a card at just the right time, or when one sees, as I have seen, a Volkswagon Golf stop instantly on the wet granite cobblestones of Prague . . . as if the mighty hand of an angel had held the car back to prevent injury to the impetuous boy of four who had just jumped in front of it from the curb?

Like you perhaps, I have also wondered at other human capacities, or the lack thereof. A lawyer friend tells me about defending a young man caught trying to steal a car from inside a locked police compound and then, on the phone, saying to my friend, "How do you think we should plea?" Another lawyer friend tells me of three people who loaded a stolen car with stolen fur coats as a security guard across the street described the unfolding scene to the police over the telephone. "How can someone be that stupid," I wonder, I couldn't write something that funny! On the other hand, I can read in the newspaper at any time about the unspeakable evil that people do to other people day after day, in crystal meth labs, in government chambers, in back alleys, and in high-rise office towers. These human capacities—for evil and stupidity—lead one to wonder as well (although some might prefer the word dumbfounded for our responses to such behaviors as these, wanting to preserve wonder for natural or at least positive phenomena).

Give thanks that we hear about the human capacity for courage and kindness as well. Stories of personal sacrifices, courageous rescues, great gifts . . . these lift our spirits. Mother Teresa's story may have become a kind of cultural cliché, but for good reason: the world was forced to wonder at her vision for the poor. Mother Teresa serves as a public paradigm, but we all have cause to wonder at similar stories closer to home, perhaps ones in which we function as characters and not just narrators. I keep a simple, framed magazine photo of her face on my office wall to remind me daily of how she responded to her vocation. Her photo prompts me to ask, "How did she do it?" and "Why did she do it?" In a sense, that photo keeps me wondering.

In short we may wonder at lots of things. I hope we do. But I fear that our society has lost much of its capacity to wonder. I want to know where it went. And why?

NO WONDER

In part, wonder went away because of our scientific advances and our expanded understanding of how the world works. Picture this scene if you will. On a Saturday morning visit to the natural history museum, my two daughters and I stand before an animated, half-size T-Rex, waiting for its computer-generated roar and movement to begin. No other museum guests happen to be present at the moment that Megamunch (as he was known) begins to move his head, open his jaws, and fill that part of the museum with his roar. My younger daughter, four years old and terrified, instinctively seeks the assurance of my hand and the security of my leg.

Seeing her fear, her seven year old sister hugs her with one arm, and reassures her with these words, "Don't worry, Kristen, it's just a cassette." The cassette may date the story but the story's point is timeless. By age seven, what should have been a natural fear in my older daughter had disappeared because she understood how T-Rex worked. To be fair, she had witnessed his roar on previous museum visits, but even with that information in hand, her technological savvy—her knowledge of what was behind it, so to speak—reduced her awe, her capacity to wonder at T-Rex.

To understand where wonder went, we need to back up a few centuries from that 1990 Saturday morning in Regina, Saskatchewan, to the early 1600s, a time that many historians name as the birth of the modern period. Recall that, for Europeans at least, the Medieval worldview which had remained in place for several centuries had been broken by the dramatic expansion in knowledge associated with the Renaissance and the age of exploration, and by a similarly dramatic reduction in how ordinary people understand authority after the Protestant Reformation. A new world and a new worldview had opened. Scientists such as Francis Bacon, who published *Novum Organum* in 1610, and philosophers such as René Descartes, who published *Meditations on First Philosophy* in 1623, wrote about knowing and certainty so persuasively that people of all social classes began to see the world in literally a new way. Explanations of reality that had sufficed nicely for centuries proved unsatisfactory. We all recognize the gains humans have made by understanding that scientific observation (following Bacon) and rational deduction (following Descartes) are legitimate ways of gaining knowledge.

However, left to their own devices, science and rationality may become scientism and rationalism. Either way, the certain knowledge they offer has the power to disenchant—to take the enchantment or wonder out of—the world, a subject explored articulately by many others (for example, Bais, 2010; Taylor, 2011). As I write, in 2012, we have a reduced capacity for wonder, although we have not lost it completely. Still, at this point in our history, we may be more inclined to be wonder-struck by a laser show than by lightning or by the advertised capacities of the latest phone than by the intimacy of face-to-face conversation.

Science, with help from its child, technology, reduces our capacity to wonder in another way: by providing us so many ways to mediate the world we live in and thereby deny ourselves direct experience of that world. To illustrate, our forebears had a much more direct experience of home heating than we do. They chopped or bought firewood, hauled it to the woodpile and then to the fireplace or stove, and several times per day took steps to keep a fire going . . . all to avoid a more direct experience of winter. Our own experience is highly mediated: most of us pay a utility to supply us with electricity, gas or oil. We set a thermostat, perhaps with twenty-eight different programmable cycles so our house stays warm on the days when we are home and cooler when we are not home or at night. For the most part—if the thermostat is working correctly—we rarely have to think about temperature. Thanks to the furnace and thermostat, we mediate our experience of winter much more easily than our forebears did with wood heat. Thanks to the digital thermostat with multiple settings, we can even mediate the work required to run the thermostat.

Dozens of similar examples come to mind. Our shelters themselves are meant to mediate the seasons and the day's weather. We use elevators and escalators to avoid experiencing the actual height of our buildings. We use an array of electronic devices to mediate the distances over which we want to communicate. We substitute texting for face-to-face communication (or "FTF," as we now abbreviate it to mediate the time and key-stroke demands placed on us by full words). We substitute online games for face-to-face games. We substitute recorded music for music we might make ourselves. We substitute shopping for building, crafting, sewing or growing what we need. We use automobiles to mediate the time and distance involved in travel by foot. Lest we get bored during the already abbreviated time required in transport, we entertain ourselves with music. Those whose music comes from a car radio may mediate the spaces between songs by changing channels to avoid the annoyance of hearing from the advertisers who pay for the songs. We mediate our sickness with medicine and all manner of work with machines. A Luddite would love this lament so far, so let me make clear that I happily take advantage of many of these forms of mediation. My concern is that we allow too much of our lives to become mediated, even in those areas where mediating our experience offers little apparent return. And in living lives mediated to such degree, we perhaps deny ourselves many occasions to wonder.

Does all this mediation really stifle wonder? Not necessarily, but typically. I enjoy the spectacular, whether that spectacle involves the roar of race cars, a laser show or the latest computer advance. I might even admit the word *wonderstruck* into my response to the spectacular. And I confess to surviving only five minutes when I set out to finish my current basement using only a hand-saw (in an ill-conceived plan to understand better my long-dead grandfather who worked as a carpenter). But what if our culture is all *allegro* and no *adagio*? Will we lose our capacity to experience wonder in the face of silence? Given the cultural shift toward more and more mediation, entertainment and technique, if we want to recover wonder we will need to be deliberate about engaging in direct experience. Whatever aspect of daily life we think about—work, transport, food, music, and conversation—mediations offer themselves to us. If we want to recover wonder and our collective capacity to wonder, we will necessarily have to seek unmediated experiences in our own lives and in our classrooms.

Discussion Questions

Recollect a scene or vignette from your own life where you were struck with wonder. What were some of the features or qualities of this scene.

Recollect a scene where you realized that you no longer responded in wonder to a phenomenon that would have caused you to wonder at an earlier time in your life. What are some of the factors that you think led to the diminishment of wonder over the intervening years.

List some ways that you mediate your life that you could experience directly, at least on a trial basis, without too much difficulty.

Our personalities are all different. Some of us respond more easily to natural sources of wonder while others of us respond to the latest technologies. Still others become wonderstruck by conversation, music or art. In your case, what sources of wonder work most powerfully. What might we learn about God or ourselves from our individual differences in this dimension?

THE WONDER CONVERSATION

Literally hundreds of writers have addressed wonder. Indeed, the line of artists, writers, theologians, psychologists, and philosophers stretches back as far as classical Rome and Greece. Wisdom calls for noting just a few voices here. Sam Keen invited me into this conversation decades ago with his *Apology for Wonder* (Keen, 1969). In my later section on wonder in our classrooms, I will recommend this title for anyone wanting a compelling invitation to live in wonder. Paul Griffiths offers some surprising insights on curiosity and a wonderful chapter on wonder in *Intellectual Curiosity: A Theological Grammar* (2009). He sees curiosity as a needed value or disposition for doing science but distinguishes it from wonder, which he understands to be a form of awe in the face of God's creation (on the links between curiosity and wonder, see Dewey, 1935; Opdal, 2001). I think any Christian would benefit from reading Griffiths, certainly any Christian whose vocation is teaching. Although Barbara Fiand tills some of the same ground as Griffiths in her *Awe-Filled Wonder: The Interface of Science and Spirituality* (2008), she makes links to mystical experience and, as she understands it, the false tension between science and faith. For readers wanting to explore this dimension further, I also recommend Deane-Drummond (2006) and Cooling (2006).

Robert Fuller has written *Wonder: From Emotion to Spirituality* (2006), an accurately-titled and quite readable exploration of some connections between wonder and spirituality. Fuller argues that wonder actually increases human sensitivity to the spiritual dimension; that is, people who wonder are more likely to embrace religious faith, an argument that should not surprise readers of this current volume. More recently than Fuller, William Brown has written *The Seven Pillars of Creation: The Bible, Science and the Ecology of Wonder* (2010). Brown examines seven different scripture passages related to the physical world and God's view of it. Anyone who resonates with Griffiths' or Fiand's work on wonder will likely enjoy Brown, as will those who love Scripture but who weary of controversies about creation and evolution.

Finally, I recommend Matthew Crawford's *Shop Class as Soulcraft*, (2009), published in Europe with the intriguing title: *The Case for Working with Your Hands, or Why Office Work is Bad for us and Fixing Things Feels Good*. Crawford gives a good deal of his effort to reminding all of us, but especially educators, that unmediated experience yields benefits to the learner. Although each day we seem to increase the degree to which we mediate our own and our students' experience with more technology, we still live in a material world and contact with that material can generate wonder. When Madonna claimed some decades ago that we live in a material world, she offended many Christians, including me, because I want to argue that our world is also spiritual, alive everywhere with the pulse of God. But

Madonna was partly right. We deal with material things all day long and we are made of material. Even our language, by connecting the words *human* and *humus*, reflects the connection the Genesis creation account makes between soil/clay (Hebrew *adamah*) and human (*adam*). I doubt very much that Crawford's book grew out of Madonna's philosophy-put-to-music, but we need to take our materiality seriously, and a great place to start doing so is between the covers of Crawford's book. To help yourself grasp his point, I recommend you get a paper edition, not an ebook.

A THEOLOGY OF WONDER

In response to my comment that I was trying to understand and write about wonder, someone suggested to me that wonder was a *creaturely response to God's created order*. I think this phrase catches the conception of wonder Griffiths builds in *Intellectual Curiosity*, which I mentioned. It also catches much of what I would say if I were to write an extended theology of wonder. Thankfully, as I noted in the previous section, several writers have capably approached that task already (as have McGrath, 2002; Sigrist, 1999).

What might a theology of wonder look like? Consider these passages from Scripture for a sampling of what its tone might be. The Genesis accounts of creation have God thinking the creation very good once it was complete (Genesis 1:31). In the story of Job, God's creative wonders actually constitute a theme, with animals, birds, plants, fish, stars, and seas all apparently pointing to God's power and, in some cases, even aware that God does marvelous things beyond human understanding (Job 9:10). In Psalm 139, we discover a Psalmist in awe of God's work. On this account, God knows the details of our lives before conception; we are fearfully and wonderfully made (Psalm 139:14). Neither do the New Testament writers shy away from such themes. At least one author finds wonder as a motif in the Gospel of Mark (Dwyer, 1995), and the Apostle Paul stands in awe of Christ, in whom and for whom the whole created order exists, and through whom it holds together (Colossians 1:15–17). In fact, on at least one account, wonder runs right through Paul's theology (Davis, 2006).

Without overwhelming my readers with more references, let me suggest that the biblical writers cited here invite us to make an appropriate creaturely response to God's power and the Divinely created order. Indeed, I want to live my own life as just such a creaturely response. And I certainly want my classroom—whether in a public or a faith-based setting—to be a place of invitation for others to make the same response.

CREATING SPACE FOR WONDER IN OUR CLASSROOMS

In this section, I want to suggest several conditions that we will likely need to meet if we want to create a learning/teaching space where students are invited to wonder. Mixed with these conditions, I want to suggest strategies that teachers might use to make the invitation to wonder more clear to their students.

Passion, and Living in Wonder Ourselves

Teacher passion is an obvious precondition for students to hear an invitation to wonder. At some time, we have all used the word *passion* to describe a teacher's enthusiasm for her subject. And we often describe such passion as *infectious*, knowing that students take their cues from their teachers. A resigned or bored teacher produces bored and resigned students. An enthusiastic or passionate teacher leaves a few students scratching their heads but inspires most students. Think of how many adults attribute their first stirrings to become a chemist, writer, lawyer, teacher, botanist, or doctor because of a passionate teacher. Some educators have tried less effective ways to inspire students. Yelling about the importance of a subject, for example, or developing an intimidating course syllabus both have the opposite affect on enthusiasm from that intended by the teacher.

If we want to teach in classrooms characterized by wonder, we will need to live in wonder ourselves. I recognize that doing so is hardly a checklist item like renewing a car registration. But we can take steps. For starters, I think reading Sam Keen's *Apology for Wonder* would help people recover their capacity for wonder. I recommend it without reservation to any educator at any level. Second, we may have to discipline ourselves to take some time every day simply to be quiet. The little research on wonder we have seems to show that people are not usually wonderstruck unless they have predisposed themselves by cultivating habits of stopping, seeing, and hearing. I would not dare suggest that we all stop in the same way; out of necessity we will find different forms. While the forms may differ, the necessity remains common for all of us.

If we are to create a space in which our students know that they can be wonderstruck and if we have found ways to open ourselves to wonder, then we will need to let our students know about the things that lead us to wonder. We will need to show and tell. I think of an English teacher who told of her own excitement and ongoing education by asking her students this rhetorical question every day, "Do you know what I learned on the Internet last night?" She would then proceed to tell them. This same teacher created such excitement about Jane Austen's *Pride and Prejudice* that a class of high school seniors memorized one of the dances from the Netherfield Ball, as portrayed in the six-part BBC production with Colin Firth. As a surprise gift, they danced it for her at their own graduation. What teacher receives a gift like that from students? In this case, one whose own constant wonderment at Jane Austen rubs off on all around her. For that matter, what kind of students get swept away by Austen to that degree? In this case, the students whose teacher allows her own capacity to wonder to show.

Obviously, we don't all care for Austen to the degree that my friend cares for Austen. But the point of my story applies: we will need to incorporate occasions for and invitations to wonder into our curriculum, instruction, and, yes, even assessment. Some may respond to my assertion that such incorporation might be easy in a subject such as science where resources are available with titles such as *A Head Start on Science: Encouraging a Sense of Wonder* (Ritz, 2007; Van Noy, 2008; Vygotsky, 1978) and where the subject matter is inherently amazing . . . think the endocrine system or galaxies. Actually, subject matter is a diversion here. The key is in how we set or frame the subject matter. There are teachers who could make the endocrine system or galaxies boring and there are teachers who can make prepositional phrases interesting. My point is that we can invite our students to wonder in every subject area, not just the first one any one of us thinks of as more inherently capable than another of inducing or inviting wonder. And I believe that teachers who express passion about the curriculum contents and who live in wonder themselves sweep the students along with them.

Questions and Inquiry

Teacher passion and wonder alone will not generate wonder. Great instruction requires great questions, whether in a textbook, on a website or handout, or in class or small-group discussion. The great question must meet several criteria. To generate critical thought, the question must require students to draw on an array of knowledge. Note the difference between (a) "What year did the Berlin Wall come down?" and (b) "How do you think secondary students on both sides of the wall would have responded to changes in their society that resulted from the collapse of the wall and what it symbolized for the formerly divided city and country?" While I hesitate to offend my readers by calling your attention to the obvious dif-ference between the two kinds of questions, I must point to two facts. First, the culture of assessment within which most teachers now do their work rests on a layer of assumptions, including the assumption that worthwhile learning must be measurable. A computer can grade 20,000 students' an-swers to question "a" above faster than teachers can grade 20,000 students' answers to question "b." In short, we educate in a culture of assessment. But second, as educators in a culture of assessment, we often cave too quickly; we blame the policy-makers (perhaps rightly) but we stop looking for ways to ask question "b." I believe that students can learn the answer to question "a" and still engage critically with deeper questions.

I hesitate to point to the obvious difference between the two questions for a second reason, one that should sober us all. Many teachers do not themselves aim to—or perhaps possess the skills to—create questions like question "b" above, questions that require critical engagement. As a result of these two realities (and likely others), classrooms and students want for wonder. And they will continue to want for wonder as long as policy makers continue with politically-popular understandings of assessment and teachers lack the skills and dispositions to move students into modes of critical engagement, what Vygotsky (1978) called the zone of proximal development.

Great questions must meet a second criterion: the teacher cannot al-ways know the answer. Some readers will disagree with me immediately, but please let me nuance my claim. A teacher will obviously know what year the Berlin Wall fell, what letter comes next in a Kindergarten student's surname, and a thousand other facts. But even on "what letter comes next?" (where the teacher knows the answer) the good teacher will proceed with the student—will construct a learning situation—where the student has to think. For example, the teacher might say, "You suggested that the letter 'p' comes next in your name. Let's sound it out with a 'p' to discover if that's right."

The social studies teacher in my scenario likely has some pretty good ideas about why the Berlin wall came down and maybe about some of the ways that adolescents responded to changes in post-unification Germany. But she still plans her instruction so that students need to think deeply to answer her questions. We know that some teachers, faced with the question of adolescents' responses to the fall of the Berlin Wall, would provide a bulleted list to their students rather than ask their students to work out those answers through research, imagination, writing, and discussion. We can all live in hope that all teachers would become creatures of pedagogical imagination. We can even hope that many teachers would develop the courage and skills to ask the students themselves to identify what questions the collapse of the wall must have raised for Germany, that is, to lead their students into enquiry learning. Such teachers will find both encouragement and help in the writings of several who have addressed the connections between enquiry learning and wonder (Ciardiello, 2003; MacKenzie, 2001; Siejk, 1995; Stark, 2005).

Direct Experience

I begin dealing with the matter of mediated and direct experience by briefly mentioning two educators who have written before me about the importance of direct experience and materiality. Recall that Maria Montessori included the sense of touch as an important component in learning (Montessori, 1912). Dewey repeatedly called for students to have direct experience of that which they were studying (Dewey, 1902, 1938). We may awaken a dormant part of our students' consciousness if we build direct experience into their schoolwork. If, as Christians believe, people are spiritual as well as physical, we may thus recognize, serve, and awaken the spiritual dimension. Consider three examples. Without a trace of Luddite lament in my suggestion, let me recommend that we could offer some measure of mental and physical health to our students by planning school activities that cannot be completed without face-to-face contact. For secondary and post-secondary students especially, group work often means simply dividing work up and emailing sections around (or using wiki space) until the project is complete. No conversation is required once the initial face-to-face meeting ends (and sometimes even that meeting happens by email). What is the direct experience in this case? It is conversation, unmediated by keyboards and screens.

A teacher told me about a social studies unit on the supply chain. The students' task was to find out where things came from, in this case, food. Students visited farms, processing plants, warehouses, and retail stores to trace how their food moved from ground to table. They had to bring arti-facts from each stage of the process, requiring that they not just watch and take notes. According to the teacher (who uses this unit annually), students report understanding their food in a whole new way. They realize year to year that the food supply chain has more parts to it than they knew. They learn that whole communities thrive (or fail to thrive) where food grows. They learn that many truck drivers have children in school, some taking the same social studies course. And so on. Her point is that they do field research (in both senses) and, as a result, they feel like they have more in-timate knowledge of the food that ultimately ends up on their table. They know it doesn't simply come from the store. They have direct experience.

Let me tie these examples to wonder. Regarding conversation, when students sit down to talk face-to-face they may discover the richness and magic, if I may call it that, and some of the difficulties of what humans until our own time have always known about conversation. In the second case, they will certainly experience surprise at some of the complexities in getting food to their table. In this regard, I recommend "Walking into Wonder," a good article that lays out steps for teachers to plan and lead what the author calls observation walks with classes (Rothschild, 2004). As Rothschild describes observant walking, it can be adapted for different grades and for most subject areas.

The Contradictory, the Unexpected, the Spectacular, the Contrast

The above remarks notwithstanding, teachers will still need to look for the amazing in our curriculum contents. For some of us, that may require a new mindset. But let me name some categories that may aid our think-ing. How about the contradictory? Why do people say one thing and do another? Why can two innocuous or beneficial elements, carbon and oxy-gen, produce a deadly compound, carbon monoxide? How can something good—salt—break down into a dangerous metal (sodium) and a poisonous gas (chlorine)?

How about the unexpected? Why do moto-cross racers—when they are in the air—turn their front wheel the opposite direction from where they are heading? Why does the Mercator map look like it does if Greenland is actually nine percent *smaller* than the Democratic Republic of Congo? When I taught secondary social studies, I regularly built into my courses a visit to globalrichlist.org, a site where anyone can compare their annual income to the rest of the world. Just as regularly, students would report to me, "I had no idea that my $1000.00 annual earnings put me in the top 44% of the world by income." I welcome you, my readers, to type your own (modest) educator's salary into the dialogue bar on their site right now. Does the unexpected produce wonder? Yes, of course.

For many, the spectacular induces wonder. But we need to make an important distinction here. While a rock concert may be spectacular, the average school teacher lacks the budget, staff, and trailers of equipment required to induce wonder that way. And, anyway, such spectacle likely does not induce the kind of wonder I am calling for and students need. More likely, with its sensory overload, it produces a kind of frenzy (or perhaps simple amazement) more than it produces wonder. The kind of wonder I am calling for here is more likely the state we experience in the face of naturally occurring spectacles such as floods, ice storms, and lightning. Or consider waterfalls, quiet forests, or the desert. Without simply making a stipulation or declaration that this is what I mean by wonder, this actually is what I mean by wonder.

How about extreme contrasts, for example, between very large and very small? How did engineers ever succeed in building a flying robot the size of a hummingbird? Can the Andromeda galaxy really be that far away? Extreme differences between rich and poor, fast and slow and any number of other contrasting pairs can induce wonder.

The contradictory, the unexpected, the spectacular, and the extreme contrast are just some of the categories educators can employ to frame materials to invite our students to wonder. Without illustrating, let me suggest such categories as the brilliant, the counter-intuitive, or cold, heavy, strong, expensive, renewable, contradictory, unexpected, large. These are a few of the many categories we can use as we plan our instruction. My readers will obviously think of others.

As teachers who would induce or invite wonder, our challenge becomes to look at any bit of curriculum, any section of instruction, and any element of our assessment of students' work and ask if we can introduce other materials or frame the materials we have in such a way that students will be induced or invited to wonder. We also must frame our instruction in such a way that students have to find many things out without our simply telling them.

CONCLUSION: RECOVERED WONDER

Every teacher, every day, constructs a learning/teaching space of one kind or another. That space will be characterized by the kinds of qualities my colleagues and I have written about in this book or it will be characterized by other qualities. My invitation in this chapter is for all of us to live in wonder. I cannot urge that on my colleagues or readers; I can only invite. Likewise, I am limited in my own classroom to inviting and creating the conditions of invitation. But humans possess a natural inclination toward wonder. God made us that way. And so I don't see my invitation as a particularly difficult one. May God help us all to (re)discover our natural, childlike capacity for wonder, and may God give us the courage and creativity to implement the appropriate strategies so that our students sense the power of our invitation—and God's invitation—for them to live in wonder as well.

Discussion Questions

Recollect two or three scenes where you saw students get lost in wonder. What were some of the features of these scenes? Consider some of these possible qualities: curricular or extraneous and serendipitous learning; planned or unplanned by the teacher; student was alone or in a group; teacher [possibly you] was able to incorporate the experience into instruction.

Many teachers say that the culture of assessment puts them in a straightjacket, preventing them and their students from taking the time to wonder. Think about teachers you know who have succeeded in finding time to wonder, even in the current educational atmosphere. What are some of the keys to their success?

The second part of this chapter suggests inquiry learning as one way to encourage wonder. Think about one section of one curriculum with which you are familiar. Related to that curriculum, what material, activity or strategy might you introduce to invite students into wonder?

REFERENCES

Bais, S. (2010). *In praise of science: Curiosity, understanding, and progress.* Cambridge, MA: MIT Press.

Brown, W. P. (2010). *The seven pillars of creation: The Bible, science, and the ecology of wonder.* New York: Oxford University Press.

Ciardiello, A. V. (2003). To wander and wonder: Pathways to literacy and inquiry through question-finding. *Journal of Adolescent & Adult Literacy,* 47(3), 228–39.

Cooling, T. (2006). Curiosity: Vice or virtue for the Christian teacher? Promoting faithfulness to Scripture in teacher formation. In R. Edlin (ed.), *Engaging the culture: Christians at work in education* (pp. 75–89). Sydney, Australia: National Institute of Christian Education.

Crawford, M. B. (2009). *Shop class as soulcraft: An inquiry in the value of work.* New York: Penguin.

Davis, D. M. (2006). The centrality of wonder in Paul's soteriology. *Interpretation,* 60(4), 404–18.

Deane-Drummond, C. (2006). Finding wonder, seeking wisdom: Reflections at the boundary of science and religion. *Modern Believing,* 47(4), 17–28.

Dewey, J. (1902). *The child and the curriculum.* Chicago: University of Chicago.

Dewey, J. (1935). *How we think: A restatement of the relation of reflective thinking to the educative process* (2nd ed.). New York: Heath.

Dewey, J. (1938). *Experience and education.* New York: Macmillan.

Dwyer, T. (1995). The motif of wonder in the Gospel of Mark. *Journal for the Study of the New Testament,* 57, 49–59.

Fiand, B. (2008). *Awe-filled wonder: The interface of science and spirituality.* Mahwah, NJ: Paulist.

Fuller, R. (2006). *Wonder: From emotion to spirituality.* Chapel Hill: University of North Carolina Press.

Griffiths, P. (2009). *Intellectual appetite: A theological grammar.* Washington, DC: Catholic University of America Press.

Keen, S. (1969). *Apology for wonder.* New York: Harper & Row.

MacKenzie, A. H. (2001). The role of teacher stance when infusing inquiry questioning into middle school science classrooms. *School Science and Mathematics,* 101(3), 143–53.

McGrath, A. (2002). *The re-enchantment of nature: Science, religion and the human sense of wonder.* London: Hodder & Stoughton.

Montessori, M. (1912). *The Montessori method: Scientific pedagogy as applied to child education in "the children's houses"* (A. E. George, Trans.). New York: Frederick A. Stokes.

Opdal, P. M. (2001). Curiosity, wonder and education seen as perspective development. *Studies in Philosophy and Education,* 20, 331–44.

Ritz, W. C. (2007). *A head start on science: Encouraging a sense of wonder.* Arlington, VA: National Science Teachers Association Press.

Rothschild, C. (2004). Walking into wonder. *Green Teacher,* 74, 24–26.

Siejk, K. (1995). Wonder: The creative condition for interreligious dialogue. *Religious Education,* 90(2), 227–40.

Sigrist, S. (1999). *Theology of wonder.* Torrance, CA: Oakwood.

Stark, H. E. (2005). Philosophy as wonder. *Dialogue and universalism,* 15(1/2), 133–40.

Taylor, C. (2011). Disenchantment-reenchantment. In *Dilemmas and connections: Selected essays* (pp. 287-302). Cambridge, MA: Belnap.

Van Noy, R. (2008). *A natural sense of wonder: Connecting kids with nature through the seasons*. Athens: University of Georgia Press.

Vygotsky, L. S. (1978). Interaction between learning and development (M. Cole, Trans.). In M. Cole, V. John-Steiner, S. Scribner & E. Souberman (Eds.), *Mind and society: The development of higher psychological processes* (pp. 79–91). Cambridge: Harvard University Press.

8

Stewardship

TERAH R. MOORE

MY CLASSROOM IS COMPRISED of eleven eager graduate students wanting to become teachers. Each person represents a unique life story that will continue long after we part ways. They sit facing me and engage in dialogue about strategies in teaching and learning. There is something on my mind that I must share with these students. After a few minutes of basic content, I take a deep breath and plunge into the dreaded emotional abyss and share that I will leave them mid-program. Such news can be devastating and can leave a cohort, class, or faculty with a bitter sense of abandonment. Even though I hold a detailed outline, I am unable to follow it because I am drawn to my students' eyes. Instead, I bumble through the sequence of events that led me to the decision. In addition to breaking the news, I needed to instill confidence that they will succeed and finish without me, and communicate the process of my departure. When I finish, my students clap and celebrate through their tears. When the night comes to an end, I am exhausted, overwhelmed, and humbled. As I reflect about how my departure applies to stewardship, I discover that I learned something new.

Through the act of my genuine care of and for my students—they reciprocated care in my time of need. Creation care and stewardship are both cyclical and surprising. Teaching is a form of creation care; it is my career, my calling and I am fulfilled when I teach well. I have just begun to understand the wonder creation care and stewardship inspire in me. Why is it that I am satisfied and at peace when I believe I have rightly invested time and effort to care—to care for people, to care for the environment, to care about learning, and to care about teaching?

This chapter defines and discusses the concepts of creation and creation care—hence forward also referred to as *stewardship*—both from a biblical perspective and a human perspective. I explore stewardship in relationship to teaching and address challenges and biblical passages associated with caring for God's creation. The chapter will also explore how stewardship relates to teacher-student relationships in the classroom. The chapter also provides principles of stewardship in education.

CREATION DEFINED

Creation, in the context of God's purpose for creation, is the act of making something when nothing, not even time, existed. In an essay about biblical perspectives and the earth, author and theologian Larry Rasmussen (1989) defined creation in the following passage:

> It is the theological word for the totality of things (in Greek, ta panta) . . . all things except God the Creator. More precisely, all things together in relation to God. Strictly speaking, "creation" is our term . . . The verb form "creating" is common in scriptures. But a noun form used to refer to some vast entity is absent, which only underscores the Creator's ongoing creating and sustaining— indeed underscores the unfinished character of the world. (p.116)

This definition of creation points to God's character and his attributes. He is eternal. He is infinite. He is all-powerful. Significant contrast exists between the attributes of the Creator and the attributes of creation. In this context, creation is temporal, finite, and ultimately dependent. The implication is a work in progress—the unfinished character of the world maintains creation's inability to care for itself in the same manner that the Creator would care for his creation. This creating and sustaining of creation also includes the enterprise of education and the care of students.

STEWARDSHIP DEFINED

Stewardship is the obligatory concern for, interest in, or provision of all aspects of creation. Our perception of stewardship is temporal and complex. It is important to look at God's perspective about the creation. Seven times in Genesis chapter 1, God looked at his creation and saw that it was good. This divine affirmation provided sufficient reason for us to be good and careful stewards of his creation in its entirety.

The passages in Genesis indicate that God instructed Adam to exercise dominion over all creatures (1:28) and then name them (2:19–20). Adam was also to fill, subdue, and rule (1:28) but also to "work it and take care of it" in reference to creation (2:15). This latter text surely implies protection, safekeeping, and stewardship over all creation and the environment. This charge extends to our work in the classroom because both faith and professional ethics require us to care for our students even as we care about our field.

STEWARDSHIP OVER TIME

The story of the blind men who encounter an elephant acts as a metaphor for our process of defining and documenting creation care themes over time. Each man attempts to describe the elephant based on the one part. None has a complete understanding of what they are trying to describe until the end of the story. It is likewise with our understanding of creation care. Paul shares that "now I know in part, then I shall know fully, even as I am fully known" (1 Corinthians 13:12). Stewardship is not the worship of creation—rather, it is comprised of but not limited to the following: caring, protection, and preservation of all creation including ecological systems, animals, plant life, and the very earth itself. But it also extends all of humanity, and certainly to our own students.

Why do we want to protect the environment today? And why to we teach our children to care for the earth? Is it ultimately because we want to honor God or is it because environmental degradation may affect our personal happiness? This latter motive is corrupt and does not result in the stewardship God intends. An incorrect motive coupled with the action of caring for creation leads to "fix-it" approaches—not really what God intended when he commissioned us to care for His creation.

Stewardship of the earth is a complex task and the question remains, why is it so vexing and complex? We each want to invest our time and talents in the areas for which we feel the most passion. While stewardship is a collective mandate and responsibility, each of us can and should contribute out of our own specific concerns and motives, while recognizing all aspects of creation that require care.

Stewardship has taken many forms over time. This is in part because our natural impulse is to not care for creation but to make sure that we take care of self. It is from this position that we have referred to environmental stewardship as the scope of creation care. While it is an appropriate term, creation care is even greater than environmental stewardship. It is foundational and is intricately woven into every fiber of life. It even spans education and how we care for students in the classroom environment and how we teach students to act as stewards of creation.

Creation care has taken on the form of protection and preservation of animals, land conservation, and concerns of pollution. Creation care has also been seen in the cultivation of new ideas and inventions to improve the quality of life. Additionally, it has focused upon efforts to improve working conditions, slum housing, food adulteration, sanitation, and purified drinking water. Sadly, this type of stewardship tends to get cast aside in periods of war and other times when it is not a high priority. However, efforts exist that address creation care issues and at times these conversations have resulted in helpful legislation. Every passing generation has responded to the issues. But, the many forms creation care has taken on indicate mankind's general misunderstanding of careful stewardship.

The Apostle Paul, in the New Testament wrote that, "For the creation was subjected to frustration, not by its own choice, but by the will of the one who subjected it" (Romans 8:20). This indicates that something went wrong in how creation was cared for. The passage in Romans chapter 1 also points to our continuous refusal to yield to the God of the universe. We would rather worship what God has made than him. While we have a responsibility to be good stewards over that which God has made, we need to be careful that we do not become creation worshipers. Romans 1:25 describes the worship of creation. This is in great contrast to the Genesis passage, which details careful stewardship of creation. The Romans passage categorizes creation worship as a lie accepted in place of true worship of the Creator through our stewardship of his creation in contrast to the purpose of creation care.

HUMAN FAILING

Human interpretation of creation care drastically differs from God's intentions. Through our presence, our character, and our wrong intentions of dominion, we have defiled the land and made his heritage an abomination, and we have caused animals and birds to perish (Jeremiah 12:4 and 2:7). God said that because there is no one who cares, creation will become a wasteland, parched and desolate, and laid to waste (Jeremiah 12:11). We have overstepped boundaries of blessing, provision, and care into selfish desires—"Is it not enough for you to feed on the good pasture? Must you also trample the rest of your pasture with your feet? Is it not enough for you to drink clear water? Must you also muddy the rest with your feet?" (Ezekiel 34:17–18).

We are not much different than people described during biblical times. We fail because we perpetuate the disregard for the earth set in motion in the Genesis story. Old Testament prophet, Hosea, reflects this in the following verse, "There is no faithfulness, no love, no acknowledgment of God in the land. There is only cursing, lying and murder, stealing and adultery; they break all bounds, and bloodshed follows bloodshed. Because of this the land mourns, and all who live in it waste away; the beasts of the field and the birds of the air and the fish of the sea are dying" (Hosea 4:1–3). Isaiah identified similar distress, "The earth dries up and withers, the world languishes and withers, the exalted of the earth languish. The earth is defiled by its people; they have disobeyed the laws, violated the statutes and broken the everlasting covenant. Therefore a curse consumes the earth; its people must bear their guilt" (Isaiah 24:4–6). Environmentally speaking, our human nature ensures that we will naturally oppose God and will destroy creation if given our own way.

Discussion Questions

How might education influence the ways
in which we care for God's creation?

Do educators hold the power or responsibility to teach concepts of
stewardship in ways that will honor creation and care for the gifts
contained therein?

"FIX-IT" APPROACHES

Each of us is able to participate in creation care as a part of stewardship, out of our own individual talents, concerns, and influence. Not unlike the story of the blind men, each of us is able to respond to challenges and opportunities. Like the blind men, each perspective should be valued and understood; however, an overall definition of stewardship should not be limited to a single scope of understanding, and more importantly each perspective should be rooted in biblical principles. Action based on limited perspective leads to a collective "fix it" approach mentality, rather than a genuine and authentic care for creation and the humanity contained within. A few negative examples of the "fix it" mentality include medical misuse, animal reintroduction, response to pestilence, and education.

In terms of the misuse of medicine, new and improved drugs are constantly introduced to improve the quality of life. Often, unintended consequences are encountered down the road. Modern medicine has provided us with the blessing of various drugs to drop the blood pressure, but responsible use would require the consideration of why the body elevated blood pressure. Medications are available to lower cholesterol levels without thinking about why the body raised them in the first place. Modern medicine, through controlled doses of toxic drugs, is used to cover up psychiatric or psychological issues that could be caused by malnutrition or a variety of other causes. It is easy to turn to a pill instead of the cause, and this desire for an immediate fix can often cause addition problems.

European starlings were intentionally introduced all over the world, and today starlings are regarded as pests because of their huge flocks, noisy habits and displeasing waste. Starlings are typically regarded as loud, obnoxious, destructive birds that steal grain, destroy crops, and crowd out native birds. Many problems created by starlings stem from their abundant numbers. Flocks can number in the thousands and the damage they do is considerable. Starlings also create problems for livestock and poultry facilities because they contaminate food and water sources. Despite claims that the starling helps decrease bug populations, studies have shown that they are not as effective as was hoped.

Dichlorodiphenyltrichloroethane (DDT) was used in the 1930s to control malaria and typhus. In 1948, it was discovered that DDT poisoned insects and was made available for use as an agricultural insecticide. DDT production and use skyrocketed. In 1962 people began to question how releasing large amounts of DDT impacted the environment. People also questioned the logic behind releasing the chemical without fully understanding their effects on ecology or humans. DDT use in the United States was banned in 1972. Our desire for a quick answer for pest control, without taking the time to consider the impact upon creation, had unintended consequences.

A set of problems was brought about by the reintroduction of wolves. The wolves have repopulated some areas resulting serious imbalance. Wolves have not been in some of the areas in over 70 years—which then requires careful calculation and prediction of consequences. Ecologists believe that the effects of the wolf recovery are reverberating throughout the entire ecosystem, in birds, fish, insects, as well as in other plants and animal species. We must wonder if the thinking behind the program to reintroduce wolves was limited to the lone animal, or if those people involved actually considered the long-range effects of wolves moving into areas they haven't naturally roamed for almost a century. As educators, we must broaden the perspectives of every student so that they think critically about the world in which they live—not only in the classroom, but also in the larger creation.

An education example of an unintended outcome lies in the No Child Left Behind Act (NCLB) introduced in 2001. This federal law dictated revised and upgraded standards for public education and increased accountability. The intended outcome for the implementation of this law was noble; however, some make the argument that the current state of public education under NCLB mandate is dire. Many schools are unable to meet required academic Adequate Yearly Progress (AYP) to receive funding. Schools that are unable to meet AYP are publically listed and parents receive notification of the school's failure, giving them the option to transfer students to higher achieving schools. School improvement plans must be written, federal funding may be reallocated, and possible school restructure plans may be put in place for schools that do not meet AYP. While the law was intended to improve education for all students, it has in turn elevated schools with students whose performance in high-stakes testing is top-level and has demoted schools with students whose performance is less.

Each of these examples speaks to our limited perspective and not fully understanding consequences—when we have reached conclusions—often only to find out that we were terribly mistaken. The irony is that despite good intentions, and because of our finite knowledge, serious problems of pestilence, disease, death, starvation, and negative consequences still exist. Admirable intentions, good skills, and even sensitive mindfulness about the environment are not enough.

FOUNDATION FOR CARING: MY PERSONAL PROCESS

In the same way, I have struggled to define my own understanding of stewardship and continue to struggle with the challenges involved in the process. Is it possible by means of human understanding, apart from God, to effectively care for all parts of creation as God intended? Is the concept of stewardship one that will be fully implemented in our time on earth? As part of creation, do we have the capacity to care for creation as needed? Creation care is greater than concerns that go beyond degradation of earth. Who is responsible for the degradation of creation and who is responsible for the care of creation? We are. We have been given this charge, and we have missed the mark because of imperfection, short-term thinking, and greed for easy gain. Despite our imperfections, shortcomings, and limited understanding we must seek to do our part in taking care of all God has created.

But what does this look like? From where does genuine desire to care for creation stem? How are others taught and trained in authentic stewardship? What areas of creation am I charged with stewardship? This last question is an excellent starting point. My husband and I are responsible to care for the five acres of land we own; we are responsible to care for the youth we influence and the relationships we cultivate; and I am responsible for my own teaching. Care for each of these areas of creation looks like this for us:

- Our Land: In a pattern following the seasons we prepare the land by turning and tilling the soil and the fertilizer from our animals, the soil is pesticide free. When the ground is ready we plant. We tend. We harvest and we are sustained. The ground rests for a season.

- Our Animals: The basic needs of food, shelter, and water are met daily. But, the care of these animals extends even further. I seek relationship with them, I know them by name and I talk with them. Each has a voice that I recognize, each has an attribute that can be identified when time, and routine, and trust are established. Caring for my animals fulfills and renews my spirit; there is joy and commitment as I tend to their needs.

- My Relationships: The daily care and attention to my personal relationship with my Creator is the single most important relationship. Without my constant awareness and my intentional focus, it is I (a part of creation) who suffers. I tend to and invest in the relationship with my husband, an equal and reciprocated exchange of care. I care for and cultivate relationships with the youth in our church. This particular cultivation is most often a relationship that is guided and directed by me, since I do not expect that the youth reciprocate in the same manner in which I care for, nurture and grow the relationship.

- I know the individual voices of my pre-service teachers and respond to their specific needs. Creation care in education involves relationships, assignments, evaluation, and sensitivity to my student's needs and aspirations. I model ways that I want my students to teach and care for their students. The complexities and parameters of creation care grow as I work to prepare teachers to enter in the classrooms. Their ideas, their creations, their work, their individual constructions of knowledge involved in learning must all be cared for so that they can grow and thrive—all of this is part of my commission to care for this sector of creation.

Stewardship is complex and we must constantly seek God's guidance and assistance in caring for all that over which we hold dominion. My ability to care for creation is not as polished as I want it to be. My intentions are great but my results do not always match. When my intentions and motives are pure and align with the Spirit's leading, my efforts to care for creation are more effective. When my motives are self-gratifying and incorrect, I am unable to care, as I should. Questions linger: Am I doing this correctly? How will my action or inaction affect creation in the long term? How can I improve how I care for the pieces of creation given to me?

FOUNDATION FOR CARING: THE CLASSROOM

How then, do educators help students catch the vision of stewardship? Much can and does happen in our classrooms, more specifically in our K-12 classrooms. When teachers model creation care that aligns with God's directives, students, most often adopt that same trait or concept. The classroom is a very special place. It is a place where teachers influence, share, model, and shape—we teach. The responsibility of teaching is not one to be taken lightly.

The act of teaching is an intentional and deliberate process where an individual consciously and subconsciously teaches who he or she is.

Teachers who understand this concept model a foundational concept of stewardship for students. Teaching that reflects intentional concern for creation care occurs when teachers know who they are with respect to their Creator and are led by the spirit. Students learn by watching those who teach. Any teacher could carry out the following ten principles about stewardship in the classroom. These approaches provide indication of how well a teacher's motives align with God's intentions on how to care for His creation!

TEN PRINCIPLES TO STEWARDSHIP IN THE CLASSROOM

1. Clarity of identity—know yourself; know your Creator; know where your passion flows through in your own work; know your purpose.

2. Authentic understanding and ability to verbalize teaching pedagogy and philosophy.

3. Knowledge of and empathy for your students; the ability to view all students as God's precious children who he loves deeply and has entrusted to you as a caregiver for a season.

4. Purposeful plan in teaching direction, a goal—all actions and all teaching work toward this goal.

5. Understanding the need for prioritizing values and issues.

6. Firmness; fairness, and consistency in classroom discipline.

7. Consistent and clear communication of expectations.

8. Modeling care in all things: grading, planning and preparation, interactions with others, and self-care.

9. Identifying and maintaining God's perspective of stewardship and care of our world.

10. Practicing the disciplines of rest, reflection, and renewal.

FOUNDATION FOR CARING: ONE EXAMPLE OF CREATION CARE IN THE CLASSROOM

My years of teaching in the public school system and my experience in training pre-service teachers have afforded many opportunities to develop a personal understanding of the dynamics of a classroom characterized by the values of stewardship. The following example illustrates the values of creation care in a classroom setting.

Mr. Octavio (name changed to protect the identity of the teacher) is a middle school band/music teacher passionate about teaching students to engage with and understand the language of music. When I visited his classroom, he taught at two different schools and because of this he bounced between classrooms, not having a space of his own. Mr. Octavio's classroom was not defined by location; rather his students defined his classroom. His lessons completely engaged students and almost always demanded a captive audience. Mr. Octavio marched his students round and round as they clapped, stomped, sang, and played complex beats and tunes.

Mr. Octavio divided his beginning music class into five groups. Reluctantly, students moved to the assigned locations. Mr. Octavio's teacher presence commanded the stage as he confidently explained each group's task. Each of the five groups was expected to collaboratively compose a short piece based on the quarter note, whole note, eighth note, sixteenth note, and half note. Some students were unfamiliar with the content. After communicating his expectations, Mr. Octavio taught a mini-lesson on each of the notes. Students feverishly took notes as he explained; they gave special attention to the note their group has been assigned.

Groups were given fifteen minutes to collaboratively compose their piece and then they were expected to present it to the whole class. During this time, Mr. Octavio walked the room and answered group questions; he also asked each group for a trial run in his presence. Students worked diligently, they focused intently on their assignment, perhaps because they knew they would have to share their creation with others. There was not a single student in the class of nearly thirty who was off task. Mr. Octavio verbally affirmed each group for the work they had done, each member was validated for their contribution. Mr. Octavio assisted as needed—his role changed as needed, at times groups needed a demonstration of an example, or they needed the listening ear of an audience member, one group needed redirection—whatever the need, Mr. Octavio identified it and met it. Students fed off his energy as he gave pointers and provided guidance. As he worked with groups, he instilled confidence and a sense of pride in the work. Fifteen minutes quickly came to a close.

Mr. Octavio combined two of his passions—his love for music and his desire to share that love with others. His students caught the vision of the importance of learning about and caring for musical creations.

In this example, Mr. Octavio applied many of the ten principles listed earlier. He modeled creation care by caring for students (individual, small group, and whole class); caring for and knowing the musical content; caring for and tending to the construction of knowledge through planning and preparation for this lesson. Students were either able to see Mr. Octavio model attributes of creation care or they were aware of what the expectation was through communication. Students cared for and respected each other as they worked together in small groups and then whole class to create a musical piece. Students also learned to care for musical knowledge already constructed. Students took pride in the work they created. When teachers intentionally model creation care as a way of life in a way that aligns with God's directives within the classroom, a very natural and comfortable process of learning happens—and students catch the vision of stewardship.

CONCLUSION

Our approach to the stewardship of God's creation reflects our relationship with God, his world, and his will for his creation. As educators, we need to reflect this within our classroom both in content and in our commitment to educate our students well. We are making significant progress—all students can explain the "reduce, reuse, recycle" motto. Even though we struggle to understand the full foundations and implications of stewardship, this chapter may serve to point us in a new direction. Christian educators have the opportunity, as well as the challenge to lead and guide students to a full understanding of stewardship. This vision and challenge is built upon the full understanding of the nature of God and his purpose for our world, including education.

Discussion Questions

What areas of creation are you responsible to care for?

How can the vision for stewardship be taught to others?

How is a genuine passion to care for creation
as God intended instilled in others?

Who is responsible for ensuring that upcoming
generations understand stewardship?

How does putting yourself in a right perspective with God
impact the care of creation?

REFERENCES

Badley, K. (1996). *Worldviews: The challenge of choice*. Toronto: Irwin.

Bouma-Prediger, S. (1996). Is Christianity responsible for the ecological crisis? *Christian's Scholar Review*, 25(2), 146–56.

Meye, R. (1987). Introduction to wonder: Toward a theology of nature. *Tending the garden: Essays on the gospel and the earth*. Grand Rapids: Eerdmans. Historical Website: http://www.radford.edu/~wkovarik/envhist/.

Rasmussen, L. (1987). Creation, church, and Christian responsibility. *Tending the garden: Essays on the gospel and the earth*. Grand Rapids: Eerdmans.

9

Service

Rebecca A. Addleman

Say yes to everything. This was my view of service. As a young child, I learned the acronym JOY: J for Jesus, O for others, Y for yourself. I thought the command to love your neighbor as yourself meant, "put your neighbor's interests, needs, and wants before your own." So I readily agreed to service opportunities because I wanted to obey God, do the right thing, and please people—dismissing my personal level of interest in the activities. My understanding of service ballooned into serving everyone according to his or her needs, requests, and expectations. In addition, I tried to comply with the teaching of the parable of the talents by multiplying my talents rather than burying them in the ground—for acclaim as well as a desire to obey God. I was doing my best to keep God, my family, my teachers, my coaches, and my friends happy, but I was falling apart. The harder I tried to do everything right and keep everyone happy, the more my body seemed to shut down. As I began to miss deadlines, arrive unprepared, and experience conflict with my family and friends, I became more and more depressed. I couldn't meet everyone's expectations. Everything looked impossible and dark, without any hope of change.

WHY IS MY BURDEN SO HEAVY?

"Come to me, all who are weary and burdened, and I will give you rest. Take my yoke upon you and learn from me, for I am gentle and humble in heart, and you will find rest for your souls. For my yoke is easy and my burden is light." (Matthew 11:28–30)

For me, service seldom conjures images of easy yokes and light burdens. Rather, if there is a need that I can meet, I feel inclined to do so. I picture the burden that Jesus described in Matthew as a backpack. As I see opportunities to serve my family, friends, colleagues, students, church, and community, I pick up the responsibilities and place them in my backpack. At other times I am asked or instructed to pick up an act of service for reasons such as: a) it is the right thing to do; b) I have a gift in that area; c) there is no one else to do it. The numerous opportunities and expectations for service ensure that my backpack continues to fill and expand until it begins to bulge and stretch out of proportion. No one follows behind saying, "You seem to be carrying quite a few items; are there any that you can lay down?" No, we are not encouraged to remove items from the backpack until we have carried too much, too far, for too long. Only when the zippers weaken and items fall to the ground is it culturally acceptable to lighten the load. We can then claim, "It wasn't my fault. I tried to do everything that I was supposed to do and it resulted in health problems . . . lost relationships . . . addictions . . . burn out."

An essay on service could be written about multiple aspects of education. Limited to one chapter, I have chosen to focus on the teacher as an individual. What do we believe about service? Why is our load so heavy? How can we lighten our load by adjusting our perspective, waiting on God, and honoring community? Our beliefs about service direct the decisions we make and the paths we choose. What are we teaching our students about service—without saying a word?

Exploding at the Seams

Teaching is a service profession. We teach, facilitate, coach, counsel, challenge, plan, assess, grade, differentiate, document, translate, problem solve, attend meetings—professional development meetings, random required meetings, meetings for which we are reimbursed and meetings for which we are not. Our responsibilities as teachers grow with each new piece of educational legislation, high stakes test, school program, or curriculum adoption. Too often, leaders only assist us by sitting on the backpack, squeezing it like an over packed suitcase, to make room for just one more item—rather than removing an old expectation to make room for the new. As my mother wisely said, "No one is going to set boundaries for you; they will keep asking . . . and asking . . . and asking. You must decide whether to answer yes or no." However, setting boundaries is a struggle; many of us are addicted to doing what we "should" or what is "right" or what will make others happy. In the teaching profession, we are rewarded for these qualities. An unwritten expectation in educational culture is "unless we are too busy, we are not doing our jobs." We need not fret about criticism from administrators or those outside our profession, we already judge each other and ourselves by an impossible standard. We learn to prove our worth by talking about the impossible list of tasks that we must accomplish. If we have no time, no energy, and no space to relax, we cannot be criticized. I remember sitting in an awards ceremony where a woman was given a certificate to celebrate her contribution to the school. She was commended for "doing the work of two people, never saying 'no' to a request for help, and consistently staying late to accomplish the demands of the job." Yes, she was doing the job of two people—literally. One of her colleagues had quit and the school did not hire a replacement. I have to ask, is this a model of excellence and a standard of measurement that we want to applaud? Must success equate to a backpack exploding at the seams?

Tyranny of the Urgent

Although Christ's ministry was characterized by service (Mark 10:45), He did not meet every need. I am often encouraged by an insight from *The Tyranny of the Urgent* by Charles Hummel (1994). The night before Jesus was crucified, He prayed to God, "I have brought you glory on earth by completing the work you gave me to do." (John 17:4). Hummel pointed out that Jesus did not heal every illness, feed every person, or save every soul. He did not respond to every need, yet He completed the work that God had for Him. If meeting every need was not God's plan for Christ, it is certainly not the burden He has planned for me.

LIGHTENING THE LOAD: ADJUSTING OUR PERSPECTIVE

"Trust in the Lord with all your heart and lean not on your own understanding; in all your ways acknowledge him, and he will make your paths straight." (Proverbs 3:5–6)

Intellectually, we may not agree with the perspective that we must meet every need, but the guilt that we feel for saying "no" to an obvious need betrays our underlying belief. We want to please God and others, so we strive to do the "right" things. We want to be good teachers, so we say "yes" to service opportunities that support effective teaching. We want to be loyal and loving friends so we fill our backpacks with activities that "good friends" do. But when do we take time to question the activities that our culture equates with being good teachers, good parents, good friends? When do we stop—and listen for the Holy Spirit's guidance about which items to pick up and place in our pack?

Filling My Backpack: Choosing the Good Part

Mary and Martha

We can be blinded by the assumption that because it is good, it is God's will. But in the example of Mary and Martha, Mary could have easily chosen to be a good sister and hostess by helping Martha with the preparations for Jesus' visit instead of sitting with Him and listening. Helping her sister would have been culturally appropriate, as well as the "right" thing to do from Martha's perspective, but it was not God's will. When Martha complained to Jesus about her sister's failures, He responded, "Martha, Martha, you are worried and upset about many things, but only one thing is needed. Mary has chosen what is better, and it will not be taken away from her" (Luke 10:41–42). Martha was asking Mary to pick up a reasonable act of service, but it was not God's will for her at that moment. If Mary had filled her pack with service activities that others considered right and good, she would have missed God's plan. There are abundant opportunities for service; we cannot carry them all.

Service Projects

Mary's ministry of presence can provoke disequilibrium when personal or cultural expectations place a higher value on Martha's more obvious approach to service. A few years ago during a service-learning project at a refugee center, many of my students were frustrated because they were serving as Mary instead of Martha. They felt that the time with children was wasted because it was only temporary; the footprints of their service would disappear because they were not leaving behind a more permanent contribution, such as planning curriculum for future groups or making physical changes to the facility. In *Transformations at the Edge of the World*, Smedley (2010) tells the story of a college student who had similar concerns regarding a service-learning project in Uganda. The student struggled with the village's disinterest in her work to provide health kits for needy families. Like Martha, she had taken the initiative to meet physical needs—to leave her footprint—but was dismayed to learn that the community valued her presence above her good work. Her professor wrote the following reflection about the community's views on service:

> It's not that these initiatives were not helpful, or even welcomed . . . but they were not what the community really wanted. They certainly helped for a time, but students spent all of their time at the orphanage doing good work [health kits]—and they missed out on an opportunity to practice being present and giving the children their full attention. (p. 20)

Our time is limited. If the college student in Uganda had given her full attention to the children, she would have had little time to provide for physical needs. If my students had spent their time creating curriculum and fixing plumbing, they would have sacrificed their ministry of presence. If Mary had helped Martha, she could not have listened at the feet of Jesus. Just because it is good does not mean it is part of God's plan. The space in our backpacks is limited; the choice to pick up one "good item" automatically precludes others that are equally good. This dilemma creates greater dependence on God's guidance. Because both paths are good, we must rely on God's direction to choose the "good part that will not be taken away."

The Good Samaritan

Many of us need to remove items from our packs so we have the time and energy to serve when God leads. We need to consider how many items are in our packs because of guilt, or a longing to please others, or because "no one else can do the job as well as we can," or because we think no one else will do the job if we lay it down. In the Parable of the Good Samaritan, the Samaritan exemplifies loving your neighbor as yourself. But, as Cloud and Townsend (2004) point out in their book, *Boundaries*, the Samaritan served without feeling obligated to meet the wounded man's every need. He chose to sacrifice his time and money but did not choose to cancel his journey or stay to become a permanent caregiver. We are not called to meet every need. Seeking God's perspective can lighten our load by focusing our attention on "the good part," freeing us to accomplish the work He has planned for us to do.

Filling My Backpack: God's Grace is Sufficient

Lightening our load is not only a matter of laying down the burdens we are not called to carry but also knowing which ones to pick up in the first place. What are your strengths? How has God gifted you to serve? Which acts of service feed your soul, fulfill you, bring you joy? I often wish that I had a handwritten list from God detailing the items I should pick up and place in my backpack and which ones I should admire from afar. I cannot even rely on the litmus test of strength v. weakness; God sometimes calls us to serve in areas that sharpen our strengths and at other times to demonstrate His strength through our weakness. God has placed me in many situations where I would certainly fail if left to rely on my own abilities. In these places I am reminded that He does not need me to be able—but willing, as He said ". . . my grace is sufficient for you, for my power is made perfect in weakness. Therefore, I will boast all the more gladly about my weaknesses, so that Christ's power may rest on me" (2 Corinthians 12:9).

God's Strength in My Weakness

As a college student, I served on a summer ministry team called Athletes Living in View of Eternity (ALIVE). Six of us travelled from state to state leading sports clinics at summer camps. I loved those summers—surprisingly so, since I am not an athlete. I am not even a mediocre athlete: I always hid in the outfield and ran from the baseball, I took badminton to satisfy my PE credits in college, and during the traditional summer camp hike to some horrible summit, I was always the last one to arrive—just in time to join my well-rested peers for the hike back down the mountain. From a human perspective, there was no reason that I should have been on the ALIVE team, but that is where God placed me to serve—building relationships with teenagers through running volleyball clinics, working as a camp counselor, leading worship, performing in skits, and . . . hiking. I experienced extreme disequilibrium during those summers, balanced equally by joy and fulfillment. It made no sense for God to place me on a ministry team for athletes, but if I had focused on my shortcomings and refused to pick up that act of service, I would have lost the opportunity to watch God pour out His power through my weakness.

God's Strength in Moses' and David's Weakness

Throughout Scripture, God asked his followers to serve in their areas of weakness: Moses and David illustrate two different responses to God's leading. When God called Moses to serve by leading the Israelites out of slavery, Moses focused on his own inabilities: "Oh, Lord, I have never been eloquent, neither in the past nor since you have spoken to your servant. I am slow of speech and tongue" (Exodus 4:10). God responded with a promise that I, as an introvert, have regularly claimed as my own. "Who gave man his mouth? Who makes him deaf or mute? Who gives him sight or makes him blind? Is it not I, the Lord? Now go; I will help you speak and teach you what to say" (Exodus 4:11–12). God had chosen Moses for this task and equipped him through years of preparation, but Moses chose to lean on his own understanding. Rather than trusting God's power and plan, he responded, "Please send someone else."

David answered differently. When David volunteered to fight Goliath, the people around him advised against his decision. Saul dismissed him as too young and inexperienced. David's brother questioned his motives and accused him of conceit and a wicked heart. Rather than focusing on their words or his own weaknesses, David acknowledged God's power and trusted God to direct his path. He responded, "The Lord who delivered me from the paw of the lion and the paw of the bear will deliver me from the hand of this Philistine" (1 Samuel 17: 37). He even declined Saul's armor, choosing a slingshot instead because it was familiar and comfortable. We sometimes make the mistake of thinking that we must serve God the same way others do—or the mistake of judging others when they do not serve God as we do. God differentiates. With which skills are you familiar and comfortable? How might God use those for His purpose?

Moses could see only his own weakness; David saw God's strength. I define wisdom as seeing situations from God's perspective. Once, when standing at the top of a fortress, looking down at the city I had just navigated, I was reminded that God sees the maze of streets I travel from a completely different perspective; His line of sight is not limited by the towering rows of buildings and sharp corners that block my view. When God leads us to pick up or lay down an act of service, we can trust His leading for our path—even if it lies in an area of weakness. I see only my immediate circumstances and abilities, while God sees the entire path. My load is lighter when I rest in His leading and trust His perspective.

LIGHTENING THE LOAD: WAITING ON GOD

> "…but those who hope in the Lord will renew their strength. They will soar on wings like eagles; they will run and not grow weary, they will walk and not be faint."
> (Isaiah 40:31)

As we become weary and discouraged on our journey, we long to empty the backpack completely. Most of us have items in the pack that we need to lay down, but if we are not careful, we could lay aside items that bring joy and fulfillment while clinging to acts of service that weigh us down. In his book *Walking with God*, John Eldredge (2008) states,

> Isn't this our first reaction, when life seems overwhelming—we start lightening the load, dumping cargo overboard so we don't drown? The problem is, we can dump the wrong things overboard! We think nothing of tossing over joy while hanging on to the very things that overwhelm us. (p. 200)

Waiting Renews Our Strength

When we cannot or should not remove an act of service from our pack, how can we lighten our load? While reflecting on this question, I was

149

reminded of Isaiah 40:31 and its teaching—waiting on God lightens the load. As a child, I attended summer camp. Our schedule was filled with campfires, games, special speakers, and plenty of activities to tire us out before bedtime. The most memorable activity was an annual late night challenge course where we would compete against other teams to reach the finish line. As soon as someone let go of the rope that connected our team, the entire team had to stop and wait until all hands were connected before resuming our trek through the dark. The typical team leader would wait for the signal to begin and then shout out instructions to run—through the woods, fields, ravines, and the camp pond. We would trip over each other because the rope kept us in close quarters and those who did not run fast enough were periodically trampled by the other small children on the team. After several rounds of running and trampling, our pace would slow to a walk and we would eventually straggle across the finish line, out-of-breath, wet, and tear-stained. I wanted my team to win, but I just wasn't fast enough to keep up . . . until the year that the pastor's son was our team leader. He was a seasoned veteran at the challenge course and told us that we would easily win if we followed his exact instructions. When he said walk—walk. When he said run—run. While I did not have high hopes of victory, I was encouraged by the fact that there would be walking involved. I was surprised when, after a short run through an open field or a climb out of a ravine, he stopped to give us a chance to rest. I was certain we would lose with all that walking and resting, but I didn't care—I hadn't dropped the rope once. When we finally trotted across the finish line, we were tired and wet but in good spirits. Since there were no other teams in sight, we assumed we were last. But we had crossed the finish line first.

We had achieved success by walking when our leader said "walk" and running when he said "run." Learning to listen to the Holy Spirit's guidance is essential because running at full speed at all times is not God's plan. Sometimes he calls us to walk and sometimes to wait. Maybe He asks us to stop because we have just run up the steep embankment of a ravine and we need to rest or because He knows that we need our energy for the pond ahead. Maybe He asks us to wait so that He can equip us or mold our character for upcoming tasks. Whatever the reason, He promises that by waiting, our strength will be renewed. By waiting, we will be able to walk and run without becoming tired or weary. By waiting, we will have God's strength to carry our pack rather than buckling under a too-heavy load.

Waiting Creates Space for Growth

God is not in a hurry. He sent Christ as a baby—knowing it would take 30 years before He began His public ministry. Jesus accomplished God's work during those years of waiting, even though almost nothing is recorded about that period. People often ask, "What does God want me to do?" We want to know the end of the story—become king, have a child, achieve great success. But the truth is that God's word is a lamp for our feet, with only enough light for our next step, not the entire path. Instead, we ought to ask, how will God prepare me for the end of the story through the small steps of service that I can take today? How would David's reign as king have been different if he had taken the throne immediately after being anointed by Samuel? How did waiting for the fulfillment of God's promise change Abraham and Sarah? How would Joseph's achievements have changed if he had not been betrayed, sold into slavery, falsely accused, and imprisoned while he waited for his God-given dreams to come true?

I hate waiting. I have been waiting for God's leading regarding an area of service that fills a great deal of space in my backpack. Does He want me to lay it down? Sacrifice to keep it? Recently, I sat at the top of a mountain pouring my heart out to God about this area of my life. I was confused and I wanted to run on my own strength rather than wait for His timing. He did not give me an answer. Rather, He comforted me in the waiting. I had taken my Bible with me for the hike and as I sat enjoying the snow-covered mountains towering above a deep lake and green fields, I opened my Bible and began reading the Psalms.

> Trust in the LORD and do good; dwell in the land and enjoy safe pasture. Delight yourself in the LORD; and he will give you the desires of your heart. Commit your way to the LORD; trust in him and he will do this: He will make your righteousness shine like the dawn, the justice of your cause like the noonday sun. Be still before the Lord and wait patiently for him . . . (Psalm 37:3–7a)

I could not have found a more beautiful place to be still before God. I prayed, "Thank you for inviting your children to pour our hearts out to you and for giving me such a beautiful setting in which to do it. I commit my path and plans to you. Your will be done . . . I choose to trust you with the outcome." I did not receive an immediate answer from God regarding the act of service in question. But He did lighten my load. He created space for me to reflect on His teaching, He encouraged me through His Word, and

He reminded me that I learn to trust Him more by taking one step in faith down a dimly-lit road than confidently striding toward a clearly marked destination. Does God want me to lay down this act of service? Does He want me to continue carrying it? I don't know. I do know that He wants me to wait patiently on Him and trust His plan. Waiting on God lightens my load so that when He calls me to action, I can run and walk without growing tired or weary.

LIGHTENING OUR LOAD THROUGH COMMUNITY

As I began this chapter, I described the results of my "say yes to everything" philosophy of service. I was doing my best to keep everyone happy, but I was falling apart. I couldn't meet everyone's expectations and I knew they would be better off without me. A friend shared my situation with the school counselor and I began meeting with him weekly. One day while I was slouched in his office chair with my arms crossed, I remember telling him I was ashamed that I needed a counselor because as a Christian, I should be able to solve the problem with just God's help. I do not remember his response, but I remember God's response. He surrounded me with mentors, parents, teachers, and friends who each played a role in my healing. I would not care to repeat eighth grade, but I would walk that path again to reap the results. I started to realize that God wanted a daily relationship with me now, not just an insurance policy for eternity, and Scripture began to "make sense" as if someone had translated it into a language I could understand. I also took the first steps on a path toward understanding the joy of service.

The Hands and Feet of God: Accepting and Giving Support

Community is another way that God lightens our load. Many of us learn an unwritten rule that we must be independent, relying solely on God without any help from others. Yes, God instructs us to cast our cares on Him, but He also places people in our lives as part of our healing. "Do not merely look out for your own personal interests, but also for the interests of others" (Philippians 2:4, NASB). How often do we merely "survive," clutching our independence, rather than giving and accepting the support that community offers? Last year, I chose to follow the packing advice of a travel expert and began a three-week trip with a carry-on bag—without wheels. Apparently, you can fit more in these bags and they weigh less because the frame and wheels are unnecessary. As I carried my bag through the airport, on public transportation and through town . . . after . . . town, I realized that the expert traveler must have had considerably more upper body strength than I did. As I reached the end of my trip, I began to use the shoulder strap of my bag as more of a rope to drag my suitcase on the ground behind me. As I prepared to hoist it back onto my shoulder for a trek up a few staircases in the train station, the bag suddenly felt impossibly light. A fellow traveler had come alongside and picked up the other handle to help me carry the bag up the stairs. Carrying the weight together made the task easy. She did not carry my bag for me and she did not share my load during the entire trip, but she lightened my load when I needed it most. When our burden is not easy and removing an item from our backpack impossible, God may lighten the load through the hands and feet of the community surrounding us.

The Body of Christ: Valuing Every Member

Another way to "look out for the interests of others" as well as our own is to value the contributions that we each bring to the body of Christ. In education, we are encouraged to differentiate instruction and uncover students' interests, ability levels, and funds of knowledge in order to teach all students effectively rather than teaching only to the middle. Why then, is it difficult to accept our own differences regarding service? We struggle to accept God's choice to use us differently. At times, we see the gifts that others have and want them for ourselves because their gifts are respected and valued by our culture: "If the foot should say, 'because I am not a hand, I do not belong to the body . . .'" (1 Corinthians 12:15). At other times, we struggle to allow others the flexibility to serve God in the way that He is calling them; if they do not serve the way that we do—they are wrong. If they are working harder, they are workaholics. If they are working slower, they are lazy. "The eye cannot say to the hand, 'I don't need you! And the head cannot say to the feet, 'I don't need you!'" (1 Corinthians 12:21). Paul addresses both misconceptions with the same logic, "If the whole body were an eye, where would the sense of hearing be? If the whole body were an ear, where would the sense of smell be?" (1 Corinthians 12:17).

I recently attended a string orchestra performance that provided a vivid allegory of Paul's teaching, where he states, "But in fact, God has arranged the parts of the body, every one of them, just as he wanted them to be. If they were all one part, where would the body be? As it is, there are many parts, but one body" (1 Corinthians 12:18–19). The chamber orchestra included several violins and violas, one cello and one double bass. One orchestra but many instruments—each musical line specifically written for the range and unique qualities of its intended instrument. A few times the entire orchestra played in unison, differing only by octave, based on each instrument's range. The single melody was stunning because of its brevity and unity. But if all the pieces were played in unison, the entire room would have joined the last two rows of tourists, who were sound asleep. The unique qualities of each instrument provided a variety of moods and harmonies that would have been impossible in unison. The combination of each instrument playing at the pace for which it was best suited and from the score that emphasized its strengths created a musical experience that would have been impossible with only one member of the body: violin, viola, cello or bass. God has placed each of us in the orchestra, just as He desired. Another way to lighten our load is to give others and ourselves permission to serve God according to the gifts and abilities He has given us. Each member is essential. Play the score written specifically for you—to the glory of God.

> Each one should use whatever gift he has received to serve others, faithfully administering God's grace in its various forms. If anyone speaks, he should do it as one speaking the very words of God. If anyone serves, he should do it with the strength God provides, so that in all things God may be praised through Jesus Christ. (1 Peter 4:10–11)

CONCLUSION

Say yes to everything. Not only will this philosophy eventually drown us, but it will also lead us to throw life-giving acts of service overboard while clinging to a backpack full of impossible tasks. How can we truly find joy in service instead of trying to meet every need? JOY in service is not the result of putting everyone else's needs before our own but rather counting the needs of others as important as our own. I now understand the acronym JOY as less of a hierarchy and more as the intertwined strands of a single thread. J for Jesus. Yes, we must be courageous, willing to step up and serve through our strengths and weaknesses, when God calls. We must be obedient, willing to seek and listen to the Holy Spirit's leading—walking past good activities without picking them up so that we can serve according to His plan. O for others. Yes, we must love our neighbor, willing to sacrifice and serve in settings where there may be no reward or word of thanks. We stay watchful for opportunities to serve like the Samaritan, instead of being consumed with our own interests. We accept and offer support as part of a community committed to lightening one another's loads. Yet we cannot forget that Y is for yourself. Loving ourselves means we fill our backpacks with life-giving acts of service, as we are attentive to God's call. We must guard against the busyness that turns acts of service into actions devoid of love. Because this much is true: we can serve as master-teachers who engage students, develop integrated curriculum, differentiate for every child, and create effective teaching and learning environments, but without love we are nothing (1 Corinthians 13).

Discussion Questions

What are we modeling for our students regarding service?

How do you feel when you decline an opportunity to serve? Why do people sometimes feel disobedient when they say "no" to service?

Does your backpack feel too heavy? Why? Because the pack is bursting at the seams? Because the people around you are criticizing and discouraging? Because of your own doubts and fears? Because your desire to demonstrate love overshadows your quiet discernment of God's will?

Tell a story of a time when service brought you joy.

REFERENCES

Cloud, H. & Townsend, J. (2004). *Boundaries: When to say yes, when to say no to take control of your life*. Grand Rapids: Zondervan.

Eldredge, J. (2008). *Walking with God*. Nashville: Nelson.

Hummel, C. E. (1994). *Tyranny of the urgent*. Downers Grove IL: InterVarsity.

Smedley, C. T. (2010). Introduction. In R. J. Morgan & C. T. Smedley (eds.). *Transformations at the edge of the world: Forming global Christians through the study abroad experience* (pp. 19–32). Abilene, TX: Abilene Christian University Press.

Conclusion

AMY LYNN DEE *and* GARY TIFFIN

WHILE THE COMPLEX AND vexing definition of faith and learning integration remains unclear (Badley, 2009), the conversations surrounding the topic may evoke reactions ranging from comfort to apprehension. Those teaching in public schools must separate explicit faith from teaching and learning, at least while in the classroom. Educators in Christian contexts grapple with a variety of factors from pedagogy to theology when infusing faith into teaching. For many Christian teachers, not a day passes without the question, "How will God guide me in helping these students today?" Responding to students with grace and care, while providing an environment of wonder, may satisfy the question of how to integrate faith and learning in classrooms today. Qualities deep within one's heart, characteristics taught and embodied by our ancient mothers and fathers, and those values we attach to our faith provide far more influence upon a student than a Bible verse superfluously attached to a lesson. The previous chapters have developed biblical themes and values as operational strategies for enacting foundational Christian qualities within a classroom and have presented the readers with personal accounts of how faith has influenced and shaped teaching.

Christian educators act as a bridge between culture and faith. We are called to help students frame the way they observe and react in the time and culture in which they live. Culture and faith can inform each other, and in a era when technology and Hollywood offer a disproportional amount of informing and shaping, Christian educators hold tremendous power to help all students question deeply who they are as humans and how they might introduce new knowledge and insights into their own faith development.

Through the value of care—seeing that in action through a teacher or school system—students connect that biblical theme to thought and action thereby creating the capacity to serve each other and their community which in turn, shapes culture.

A cycle of goodness follows purposeful attention to biblical principles, whether they are overtly practiced in Christian schools, or cloaked in the pretense of good citizenship or character education. Given the increase in service learning projects required for high school graduation from a public institution, one can hardly argue that the themes presented in this edition belong exclusively in the private setting. Furthermore, the increasing focus on environmental issues, from the pulpit to politics, has placed unprecedented focus upon creation care. Our students understand the connection between daily choices and long-term effects on our community and God's creation.

Discernment, also called critical thinking in many secular classrooms, demands the first line on the list of educational goal for students, but discernment also allows administrators and other leaders to make decisions that serve schools well. Deep questioning and meaning making through various lenses, including faith, ignites a sense of wonder and causes deeper thinking at the analytical level in the taxonomy of learning. In a community of learners where active and critical interaction between content, culture and faith occur, true learning follows. Hughes writes that if students find his courses "stimulating and provocative, they must credit the Christian faith, for the Christian faith has given me not only the courage to teach, but also the courage to take upon myself the contradictions and the ambiguities that teaching inevitably entails" (2005, p. 72). Discernment, as a quality and a skill, allows students to deduce, understand, and consider the underlying truths about how they know what they know. When used well by school leaders, discernment precedes decisions that benefit stakeholders and enhance student learning.

Faithful teaching does enhance the learning experiences for all students and when teachers are willing to examine their actions and practice in light of biblical themes and values, learning becomes meaningful and lasting. Often that learning goes beyond the formal educational process. All educators serve as role models and the experiences we provide for our students shape who they become and how they view life around them. A community of joy and hospitality encourages positive dispositions of the heart, mind and spirit. The charge and responsibility of developing the hearts, minds and spirits of those who enter our classrooms, and the magnitude of the call to teach these students, requires nothing more than God's blessing by way of these biblical themes. Have we included all biblical themes used by Christian educators? Absolutely not. Some readers will have noticed that love, kindness, humility and, a favorite, justice, have been left out. They remain for a second volume.

REFERENCES

Badley, K. (2009). Clarifying "faith-learning integration": Essentially contested concepts and the concept-conception distinction. *Journal of Education & Christian Belief,* 13(1), 7–17.

Hughes, R. T. (2005). *The vocation of a Christian scholar.* Grand Rapids: Eerdmans.